DARK PSYCHOLOGY
AND
MANIPULATION

The secret of influence and manipulation of people, persuasion and body language

By

DARRELL KOERS

© Copyright 2020 by   Darrell Koers

All rights reserved.

Page Intentionally Left Blank

TABLE OF CONTENTS

INTRODUCTION

What if I told you that you could get what you want in life? You wouldn't believe me, would you? But it's true. You have the power to get what you want. One of the biggest obstacles in your way is other people. So, in this book, I will show you how to undermine and elude other people with dark psychology.

The term "dark" deters people. It is generally associated with evil. While techniques are certainly used for evil here, they are not necessarily evil in and of themselves. It all depends on how you choose to use these super-powerful mind control and influence techniques. The secrets contained here are not light; you can use them to control whoever you want. They are infallible and powerful. When you decide to use these methods, you will get quick and successful results.

You have a lot of power when you learn these methods. You can access the thoughts of others. Once you have this access, you can do whatever you want with someone's account. You can convince someone to believe you when you lie. You can make someone do what you want. You can even destroy someone mentally and emotionally and thus win a psychological war once and for all.

Practice makes perfect, and it is certainly essential to practice these tactics to do them well. You don't want to screw it up and show someone that you are actively trying to manipulate them. Being hidden is key to the success of the skills discussed here. However, sometimes you have to walk before you run, so it's perfect if you want to start with the more advanced tactics covered.

First, we will discuss the secrets of human psychology, which will help you learn how to use the methods described here. You must understand the inner workings of the human mind to manipulate it. You can't expect to manipulate people if you don't know how their minds work. A good manipulator is a home psychology specialist. This shows how most people work and how you can use basic human psychology to your advantage.

We will talk about how to crush enemies. Psychological warfare is an ancient method of using human psychology to destroy enemies. It is useful to know psychological warfare because it works. But it is also completely legal. You will get away with psychological warfare, while the use of violence can land you in jail.

We also cover Dark NLP. NLP is a very successful way for other people to like you and do what you want. Dark NLP goes one step further by learning how to use NLP methods to get people to do bad things for you or to fool and fool people easily. Because NLP works, dark NLP is a surefire way to carry out dark psychology on people.

CBT is another thing we cover. CBT is cognitive behavioral therapy and is a favorite among therapists because it works so well. You can use dark CBT to convince people to change their behavior and think against their will. You can shape people into anything you want with dark CBT.

We wouldn't be an excellent book on dark psychology if we didn't cover manipulation and persuasion topics. Getting what you want in this world is essential. People will often tell you no. But if you know how to manipulate and convince, you can always get people to say yes quickly.

Mind control is the last resort for dealing with people who don't want to do what you want. Kamikaze's brain control is a great way to make people bend to your will and become whoever you want.

If you want to lie, the biggest problem is getting caught. Getting caught up in a lie is a terrible way to lose credibility and damage your relationships. You may even lose your loved ones if you are caught lying. Learning to fool even a cunning FBI interrogator can help you avoid being caught while you lie. We will also teach you always to erase your tracks to get away with everything you do.

Getting people to like you is the best way to start with a head start in the world. You won't do well or be successful if people don't like you. You can use various psychological tricks and methods to make people like you.

Finally, we will talk about creating a nice facade. If you want to use dark psychology, you cannot have it clear. Do you remember I told you that it is essential to be hidden and be discreet? You have to learn to make a facade that takes care of it.

WHAT IS DARK PSYCHOLOGY?

Psychology underpins everything in our lives, from advertising to finance, crime to religion, and even from hate to love. Someone who can understand these psychological principles is someone who holds onto the key to human influence.

Learning all of the different principles of psychology is not necessary. Start with the lessons in these pages, and you'll have a solid foundation. You have to be able to read people, understand what makes them tick, and understand why they may react in ways that may not be normally expected. And even then, you may need to spend time taking classes and reading through countless books to gain a complete understanding.

So, if only a few people understand psychology and how the human mind works, why is it so important to know what this is? It is because those who do know what it is and how to use it can choose to use that power and that knowledge against you.

While some people are going to use these dark psychology tactics to harm their victim, there are times when you may use these tactics without the intent of negatively manipulating another person. Some of these tactics were intentionally or not added to different variety of means that could include:

- When you were a child, you would see how adults, especially those close to you, behaved.

- When you were a teenager, the mind and your ability to understand the behaviors around you expanded truly.

- You were able to watch others use the tactics and then succeed.

- Using the tactics may have been unintentional in the beginning, but when you found that it worked to get you what you wanted, you would start to use those tactics intentionally.

- Some people, such as a politician, a public speaker, or a salesperson, would be trained to handle these types of tactics to get what they want.

Dark Psychology Tactics That Are Used Regularly

- Love flooding: This would include any buttering up, praising, or complimenting people to get them to comply with the request that you want. If you want someone to help you move some items into your home, you may use love flooding to make them feel good, which could make it more likely that they will help you. A dark manipulator could also make the other person feel attached to them and then get them to do things they may not normally do.

- Lying: This would include telling the victim an untrue version of the situation. It can also add a partial truth or exaggeration to get what you wanted.

- Love denial: This one can be hard on the victim because it can make them feel lost and abandoned by the manipulator. This one includes withholding affection and love until you can get what you want out of the victim.

- Withdrawal: This would be when the victim is given the silent treatment or is avoided until they meet the other person's needs.

- Restricting choices: The manipulator may give their victims access to some options, but they do this to distract them from the options they don't want the victim to make.

- Semantic manipulation: This is a technique where the manipulator will use some commonly known words that have accepted meanings by both parties in a conversation. But then they will tell the victim, later on, that they had meant something completely different when they used it.

- Reverse psychology: This is when you tell someone to do something in one manner, knowing that they will do the opposite. But the opposite action is what the manipulator wanted to happen in the first place.

Who Will Deliberately Use Dark Tactics?

Many different people may choose to use these dark tactics against you. They can be found in many various aspects of your life, which is why it is so important to learn how to stay away from them. Some of the people who can use some of these dark psychology tactics deliberately include:

- Narcissists: These individuals are going to have a bloated sense of their self-worth, and they will need to make others believe that they are superior. To meet their desires of being worshipped and adored by everyone they meet, they will use persuasion and dark psychology.

- Sociopaths: Those who are sociopaths are charming, intelligent, and persuasive. But they only act this way to get what they want. They lack any emotions, and they are not able to feel any remorse. This means that they have no issue with using the tactics of dark psychology to get what they want, including taking it as far as creating superficial relationships.

- Politicians: With the help of dark psychology, a politician could convince someone to cast votes for them merely by convincing them that their point of view is the right one.

- Salespeople: Not all salespeople are going to use shady tactics against you. But it is possible that some, especially those who are really getting their sales numbers and being the best, will not think twice about using dark persuasion to manipulate people.

- Leaders: Throughout history, there have been plenty of leaders who will use dark psychology to get their team members, subordinates, and citizens to do what they want.

- Selfish people: This could be any person you come across who will make sure that their own needs are put before anyone else's. They aren't concerned about others, and they will let others forego their benefits so that they can benefit. If the situation helps them, it is okay if it helps someone else. But if someone is going to be the loser, it will be the other person and not them.

How is dark psychology used today?

When you were a child, you saw how adults behaved, especially those close to you.

When you were a teenager, your mind and your ability to understand the behavior around you expanded.

You could see how others used the tactics and then succeeded.

The use of the tactics may not have been intentional at first, but if you find that it works to get what you want, you will start to use those tactics intentionally.

Like a politician, public speaker, or salesperson, some people would be trained to use these kinds of tactics to get what they want.

Broad, practical and theoretical observations

Murder, rape, incest, abuse are words that can cause chills. As a culture, we have imbued ourselves with opposing ideals for entertainment purposes. We sit and watch horror movies, crime shows, and reality shows that pop into deviant divers' minds. The darkness in this becomes an obsession for some, and although they do not redo the actions or prefer the actions, there is a connection that few on the outside want to acknowledge. While most people have a shock absorber on their heads, knowing fact from fiction and good from evil, some lack it.

Imagination is one thing. Combining people's worst fears to figure out which scenario might be the most terrifying and gripping is something fiction writers and creators do. However, when you observe this dark psyche in action on the screen right in front of you, the human mind specifically recognizes why the predator or villain did what they did. Some movies and books even pursue the idea of the worst human condition. Saddened and distraught, the father who witnessed his family's murders comes out of his sinister depression to devastate those who committed the deeds, to begin with. People like to take revenge for heinous acts. But doesn't that same dark psyche apply to the culprit, regardless of the reasoning behind it?

Dark psychology does not have precise goals and cares little about the reasoning behind actions. It is the actual act of manipulation, deception, and harm that weighs on the dark psyche. The idea of revenge has been around for a long time. Some important points in the story are considered a claim of honor if you have been wronged. There are still outstanding examples of the "eye for an eye" concept. The death penalty is an example of this, although its roots are broad, and it does not currently encourage private acts of one person against another. The federal organization as a whole is in charge of carrying out the punishment. But long before that, laws were established in civilizations based on the idea of revenge.

Psychological definition

The human condition is continually studied, analyzed, dissected, and used in the psychological community. Dark Psychology backs this up too. However, in dark psychology studies, attention has focused on the predator's nature versus the human condition's prey relationship. Psychologists who focus on the dark psyche shift their research to people who commit crimes or abnormal activities with little or no instinct or concern for social norms. Most people have such a buffer to protect others from these ideals, while the perpetrators lack this ability to control their most basic sexual instincts.

You may think that the basic instincts do not include the often-gruesome acts performed by someone with a dark psyche. And while you are right, there is a significant difference with the 0.01% of criminal acts carried out by dark spirits of particular importance. If you think about the most primitive man of millions of years ago, they were missing a key player that we all consider reasonable. The first primitive peoples did not have a boring social construction from birth, supplemented by religious ideals and regulated by high-functioning governments. His most primal instinct was to survive.

In a world full of dangers, both natural and nutritious, the human mind protected the body at all costs. There were very likely times when an act of manipulation and deception was committed worse in a non-convened situation. However, our brains are programmed to see danger and act or flee towards it. Survival back then had more to do with the ability to fight animals and find food, water, and shelter. There were no other social norms.

Since our brains are the same brains that were also inside the Neanderthal man, our perception of danger is the only thing that has changed. In a world where almost everyone has food, water, and shelter at their disposal, the fight for those types of situations is lower. In today's society, we see the instinct of survival manipulated into a course where we fight for more, better, and more. Frequently the crimes committed outside of the realm of revenge or the .01 percent are based solely on those theories.

EMOTIONAL INFLUENCE AND MIND CONTROL

What Is Emotional Influence?

Dark psychology always utilizes some form of emotion to achieve its purpose. Therefore, it is only essential if we begin by defining emotional influence. In the most straightforward language, the psychological impact is the deliberate attempt by an individual or group to affect the feelings and thoughts of another in a humorous way such that the person is being manipulated does not realize it.

An emotional influence that occurs under dark psychology is malicious, and, thus, the manipulator always tries to remain discreet. In short, they will try their best to hide the true nature of their actions or intentions. If the influence succeeds, the victim(s) will never know that they have been manipulated, nor will they understand how the impact occurred. They might never understand the motivation of the manipulator. We can define emotional influence as a psychological silent bomber who successfully avoids defense and detection until it is too late.

The influencer in this form of manipulation focuses primarily on the emotional aspect of their target. Other types of manipulation might target the willpower, beliefs, and behavior, but, in this case, the emotions are the end game. The influencer may target the emotional aspect since they understand that they can interfere with all the other elements of the victim's personality by manipulating it. Interfering with a person's emotions is like puncturing their jugular vein. In a nutshell, if a person is in charge of their feelings, they are in full control of their personality and life in general.

If we were to map emotional influence onto real life, relationships would suffice as a potential spot to find it, owing to the number of feelings that connect two people. A controlling partner in a relationship will possess ulterior motives, most likely acquiring leverage over the other. To receive this, they bring up situations that make the other partner feel guilty or sympathetic. Since the other partner already feels like they have wronged the manipulator, they become easy to control. Worse still, they might remain in that situation for a long time without realizing that their lives are being controlled by the very same person they are feeling sorry for.

What Is Mind Control?

The concept of mind control has existed for as long as psychology has been studied. You have probably overheard a person express their fascination or fear concerning what would happen if there was ever a chance that someone was able to control the minds of others and make them follow his or her commands. Similarly, there have been multiple conspiracy theories about influential people or authorities utilizing their positions to force small groups of people to do certain things. There have even been court cases where the accused people blame "brainwashing" for causing them to commit their crimes. Collectively, these three examples tell us that people understand that mind control is real.

However, the form of mind controls that people seem to define is that which has been portrayed by the movies and media. Which, unfortunately, is just but the tip of the iceberg. Mind control exists in many forms, and people appear to understand very little about it. It pushes the need for an accurate understanding and description of what exactly is mind control. If we take the words of psychologist Philip Zimbardo, mind control is defined as a process whereby the freedom of action and choice of an individual or a group is compromised by agencies or agents that distort or modify motivation, perception, behavioral and cognitive outcomes. In summary, mind control is a system that disrupts a person or group at their core, that is, the level of their identity (which includes behaviors, decisions, preferences, beliefs, and relationships, to mention but a few) and creates a pseudo personality or pseudo-identity.

The above descriptions make it clear a person might be wrong to assume that they are forever in charge of their actions and thoughts. By now, you should already know that our minds are not solely at our discretion since they are susceptible to influence and control. Let us take a typical example. When you are watching an emotional movie, the directors utilize camera shots, lighting, color, music, and other enhancements to control your emotions. In as much as you are aware that what you are watching is not real, your brain still plays along, and you find yourself engrossed in the movie.

Now, think about it; if your brain can respond to a prompt which it clearly understands is not real, how would it react to hidden (covert) prompts? This brings us to covert mind control, which is the form of mind control where the victim is not aware that some distortion is being applied. Hidden mind control is the most brutal form of power known to psychologists today. It is because if a person realizes that they are being controlled, they can try to escape the situation, unlike in covert mind control, where one never gets to know it. The controller takes full charge and might drive the victim to destruction without them realizing it.

Mind control can be ethical or unethical. You might wonder how having your mind shaped by another person can be useful for you. Well, an excellent example of moral mind control began when you were growing up. When your parents were bringing you up, they applied a lot of mind control. In fact, you are the person that you are today because of this mind control. Most of the beliefs, values, and behaviors that you possess, though you might have altered some, were passed onto you by your parents. Let's get a little more practical: when you wake up, your immediate actions include brushing your teeth, taking a shower, jumping into fresh clothes, applying makeup, and having breakfast before anything else.

The Process of Mind Control

A mind controller approaches the victim with the sole intent of cloning themselves, which is making the other person think like them. This is a complicated thing to do, so, to achieve it, one has to possess an inflated ego, lack doubts about themselves, and have a high sense of entitlement. All of us are susceptible to manipulation, and what matters is how much effect the mind control will have on us.

Psychologists studying mind control have found out that the entire process seems to adhere to a typical structure. This conclusion was made after a study was conducted on multiple marketing and networking companies which used mind control to persuade clients to purchase their products. One of the outstanding similarities is that all new members joining the companies underwent a pre-planned training on how to recruit more people and convince potential customers to buy their products.

Step 1 – Understanding the target

Before anything else, the manipulator will seek to establish a bond or connection with their potential victim. Good intent, or friendship, will be the first step because it makes the victim lower all their social and psychological defenses. Once the controller gains the target's trust, they start reading them to devise the most effective method to invade them. The reading aims to tell whether their victim is susceptible to their manipulation. Like any project manager, they do not like wasting time on a subject they suspect, which might outsmart them and lead to failure.

Multiple clues are used to scan the victim. They include verbal style, body language, social status, gender, emotional stability, and so on.

A person's traits can be used to decode the strength of their defenses. All this time, the manipulator will be asking themselves questions like, "Are you introvert or extrovert?" "Are you weak?" "Are you emotional?" "Are you self-confident?" Humans give a lot of information about themselves when interacting with each other, which the controller knows all too well. From these signs, they can quickly tell if the person is cooperating. They will look at body posture and immediately analyze the victim. Excess blinking might mention that a person is lying. Arms folded across the chest might show a lack of interest or insecurity. Taking enormous strides while walking might portray fear. As you can see, the body releases so much data at any given time that it is essential to be aware of the signs that you are giving out.

When the attacker has collected enough data from the target, they now understand their interests, strengths, weaknesses, routines, and so on. Using this information, they can decide on an entry point, which will allow for easy and accurate manipulation.

Step 2- Unfreezing Solid Beliefs and Values

Each one of us has some beliefs and values engraved deep within. Most of them are the principles that were instilled in us since childhood, and others have been acquired from experiences are we grow older. We rarely let go of them but revise them as we proceed. Most of them are what make up our identities, so we do not like them being interfered with. If, at any point in time, these principles are threatened, contradicted, or questioned, our natural reaction is to defend them through all means possible. However, if a good-enough reason is given to us, we voluntarily ask them ourselves; we undergo a process known as "unfreezing."

Tons of reasons can lead us to unfreeze: a breakup, the death of a loved one, religious interference, getting evicted from our houses, to mention but a few.

Step 3 – Reprogram the Mind

The mind control process seeks to separate the target from their initial beliefs and begin reprogramming their mind. The reprogramming is meant to install the manipulator's beliefs and values into the victim's account. Apart from distancing the fundamental principles, the controller also tries their best to make them look wrong or harmful, or the cause of past mishaps in the victim's life. If the victim absorbs this reprogramming, their defense is literally lowered to zero, and they now become a robot that is ready to accept any operating system that is offered.

During the reprogramming phase, the attacker will try to ensure the victim has minimal contact with the outside world. They make everyone else to appear insignificant to the victim because this raises their opportunity to deposit their malicious principles into them. This behavior is typical in cults, which are mostly crafted to sway their followers from mainstream human life. Some sects go as far as controlling the food intake of their followers as a way of weakening them.

The psychology behind this idea is that a weak person will always turn to the person they feel has the power to protect them or alleviate their suffering. The same happens in relationships, where one partner plays the controlling role, and the victimized one has no choice but to adhere to the other.

Once the victim has been reprogrammed, the manipulator moves into the final phase of the mind control process known as "freezing."

Step 4 – Freezing the New Beliefs and Values

Once the victim has been fed with contrasting principles by the offender, the offender uses tactics to cement the new beliefs into their brains. This is what psychologists call "freezing." The freezing bit is necessary because the controller is aware of the person's original ideas that might clash with their first ones. As such, they need to force the victim to choose their malicious principles over their old ones. To do this, they might apply any of the following methods.

One of the methods is using the reward/punishment approach. When the victim acts according to the manipulator's demands, they are rewarded. Hopefully, you see the similarity between the freezing process and dog training. The dog is given treats when it follows the trainer's instructions. The trainer aims at solidifying the new skill in the dog by rewarding it.

TIPS FOR DARK PSYCHOLOGY AND MANIPULATION

Have you ever thought about using psychology in your daily interactions with others? You don't need a psychological education, nor do you need the ability to read minds. In our countless interactions with friends, colleagues, and superiors, we can manipulate the situation and take advantage of these social exchanges.

When I say manipulate, I don't necessarily mean it in a negative sense. Manipulation can be used for improvement: convincing someone to take a vacation, or doing everything you can to get that promotion. Below are several ways that mere awareness of our interactions' psychology can help us more than we hope.

The easiest way to manipulate someone is to play with their emotions. If you can guide someone to feel a certain way and benefit from it, your work is done here. To be successful every time, you must choose a goal that doesn't have much control over its own emotions. Fortunately, such people are easy to find. You need to know when to shed a tear if necessary and when to lose yourself in anger. It depends on the situation in which fear or sympathy is aroused.

When we hear people manipulating, the first thing that comes to mind is that they are psychopaths and narcissists who want to spread evil. There is a fine line between manipulation and being mean. When someone is preventing you from achieving something you want, manipulation is very helpful. If you're still the good guy, people will keep pulling the sidewalk.

Manipulation only works if the other does not even understand that he is being manipulated. You don't want to get caught manipulating people. Usually, we hear this: that manipulating people is a bad thing. Yes, if it is too much. Don't feel bad; if you want to learn to manipulate people to survive, it's always worth it.

1. Use non-verbal communication for your potential benefit

How the cerebrum animates physical developments and reactions during the day by day associations is practically wild. This sort of development can impart numerous signs to the individuals around you. Am I not catching that's the meaning? It implies that you can utilize non-verbal communication to comprehend things that words don't tell you, or even influence someone with more than just words.

I'm sure you've heard that 90 percent of communication is non-verbal (hard to believe, but 93 percent actually), which means a lot can be lost in our interactions just because we folded our arms for that one. Promotion while you looked at the ground.

Learning to read body language is just as important as conveying it correctly: it will tell you if someone agrees with you, actively participating in what you say or even if they think you are a complete idiot. By constantly picking up on others' body language, you can improve your skills and identify opportunities and dead ends for each interaction.

By doing things like imitating postures, gestures, and movements, someone may agree with you. Nodding "yes" when you mean "no" maybe guilty: interrogators rely on body language to establish blame regularly. We are all animals, and we behave as such when we shed our most advanced form of communication; the trick is to use this unconscious interaction to your advantage.

Some cool facts about body language:

- Open palms create a sense of confidence: Legoland employees cannot point. Instead, they provide instructions through the use of upward hand gestures.

- Shaking hands palm down indicates dominance, and palm up indicates submission.

- When you smile in a group, the first person you make eye contact with is the one you trust the most

2. Change the perspective

Hide the reality from those you are trying to manipulate with a reality that you have woven - go to the matrix in their minds. This one is about tact, cunning, and especially rhetoric.

"My car has only x mileage, much fewer rust spots ..."

"My poor grades and my academic probation in the second year, in contrast to the better grades in my last year, show how much I have improved since then."

And the classic: "This house is a true repair house; think about the potential."

We do this every day: flip half-empty glasses on their side. Often, perspective can make a big difference in the way someone looks at something. Your descriptions can influence this perspective itself. Rhetoric is a crucial factor underlying this idea, as it encompasses many aspects beyond what was said and how it was said. It depends on the tone, content, and appeals to reason, character, or emotion. Use rhetoric to be as persuasive as possible, exaggerate when practical, and change focus when necessary.

Think about how your arguments are structured and delivered, whether they appeal to someone's emotion or logic. Sound like you know what you're talking about even if you don't? If you can't convince someone to stop wasting paper for environmental reasons, can you convince them with an impeccably logical argument that less paper means less work? Thinking outside the box and reframing a perspective on a certain situation can help you do well in seeing things for yourself. It can also take advantage of the effectiveness of any argument you make.

Some facts to put this in perspective:

- If you convince yourself that you slept well the night before, your mind will be tricked into thinking so (also known as "placebo sleep").

- The Dunning Kruger effect: smart people tend to underestimate themselves, while ignorant people think they are brilliant.

- Studies have shown that your favorite song is probably related to an emotional event from your past.

3. Use your knowledge of others

Trust people's psychological needs and use them as a pressure point. This could be a need to conform, be accepted or included, or the opposite: the need to stand out and swim against the current. The risky decision-maker may be driven to make a bad decision; the silent crowd may be discouraged from pursuing anything that takes them away from conformity comfort.

Your weakness is your strength; it's just a matter of figuring out how to use that to your advantage. Are they prone to being overconfident that can trip them up? Not sure of something that can help you make a compelling point? They all have their kryptonite.

The more you learn about a person's psychological tendencies, ways of thinking, and characteristics, the more advantage you get over your thoughts and your overall influence on those thoughts. The key to success here is knowledge. Like any other point, it may be more important to understand your bottlenecks.

Emotional Leverage: Isn't Its manipulation? In it, he provides three basic guidelines for the most success when you use someone's emotions against them:

- Be aware that your vision is the product of an emotional basis and, no matter how you rationalize your position, you cling to it for some emotional reason;

- See that if you want them to move in your direction, your job is to discover the emotional value that drives your vision: its rightful place;

- Understand that once you know your emotional sweet spot, you can develop an approach that matches his needs with yours so that both of you can feel successful.

4. Consider the right time and options

The jaguar is an efficient and calculated hunter. Ancient legacies of success and failure have given him the biological power of the great moment. He knows when to jump, when to hit harder, and when to abort its hunt.

Know when to make your moves. This is something we learn from a young age (don't tell mom what you want for your birthday if she's in a bad mood). The trick is to stay alert and keep an eye out for opportunities. For example, try asking for certain favors when someone is tired or worried (they are less likely to expend energy to disagree or reject it).

Don't force opportunities, but welcome them and keep your eyes open. If you've been waiting to deliver a speech to your boss, don't force the conversation. You may have to wait weeks before getting a good shot, but don't be left behind once you do. If we meet someone with, say, a proposal, half the battle could be won or lost, depending on their mood at the time.

Fact: Recently, a study of over 1,000 court rulings found that judges, who should be our examples of rational thinking, areas susceptible to this idea as anyone. The study confirmed that inmates are much more likely (up to 65 percent more) to be released early in the day or shortly after lunch.

Infinite possibilities

The wonders of psychology are endless. It's a field worth exploring, but it's only useful by making an effort to learn and implement it first. The ways mentioned above of exploiting psychology are barely emerging and require little more than mere awareness.

Each of the above factors is helpful in its own right. For example, kinesics (the study of body language) can turn you into a walking lie detector if you wish. If you don't want to catch others' impulses or tendencies, you don't want to expose situations in your favor; you don't realize the body language you practice and that others are sending you are becoming blind again in a very interesting way. To maximize your exchanges throughout life.

Use the fear and relief technique to deal with individuals.

This is one of the very much explored control methods that you can use to your greatest advantage. It includes playing with an individual's feelings. It can positively cause pressure and uneasiness, yet that is the thing that makes this strategy viable. So, if the individual you are attempting to control is about to give up, go ahead and give them your shoulder to cry on. You try to change their mood and leave them completely unarmed to manipulate them. If successful, your target will do what it wants.

Go from great to great.

You start by making an unreasonable request, but you must be sure that the object will reject it. Now order something you need. Since there is a contrast between the two, the object probably follows the easy request because it is reasonable. Smart, right?

Remember one thing: the success of manipulating people in certain ways depends entirely on the goals of these people (your object or objective). If people are not doing what you want them to do, it means that they changed their goals. Now you have to channel yourself towards their modified goals and perhaps change your manipulation tactics. Experts say that changing other people's goals is easier than changing your own. That's because we are designed so that others can control our behavior with simple tactics. And they can change our behavior in such a way that they can achieve their own goals with us. That is why emotional people and people who are not clear about their own goals are easily manipulated targets. If you want to master manipulating people, reading books based on psychological manipulation is recommended. It can also help you psychologically manipulate stubborn people, who are not always easy targets. Sometimes you have to be cruel to people for your benefit, which is where manipulation skills come in handy.

The importance of the word 'because.'

When requesting something you need, utilize "because" in your solicitation. It's just plain obvious, "because" has an amazing mental impact: it forces the brain to believe that there is a reason for the request.

According to Langar's research in the 1970s, when people asked to cut the line, more people agreed with the word "because" in the sentence than requests without "because," although the reason was given is the same.

You can use this to your advantage; for example, if you want to borrow money from someone, ask, "Can you lend me three dollars because I have fewer sales lately?" Use it because the other person will understand you better and feel empathy for you.

The power of the break

Have you seen how government officials and speakers use delays in their discourse? Before reporting an important decision, they take a long pause, which effectively gets the listener's attention and curiosity.

So next time, in a meeting or conversation, take a good break before announcing the most important thing to make your presentation more effective and exciting.

Check the eye color

Check the eye color when you first meet someone. Let me clarify this: eye color is not important.

While checking the person's eye color, you can maintain eye contact with the person long enough. Also, we, as a whole, have a significant eye to eye connection to assemble trust and connections.

Call by name

Would you like to build up dependable associations with others? Recollect the individual's name and when you meet them once more, welcome them by name and state "Hi Peter" rather than just "Hi." And don't stop there; recall the little subtleties they referenced in the past gathering and get some information about them.

Individuals feel significant and regarded when you recall insights concerning them. What's more, they will consequently feel associated with you.

Quiet

If you question whether somebody is deceiving you, remain still and keep in touch when they get done with talking. The quietness and your desire for more data will lead you to reality.

At the point when we power somebody to come clean, they will make up lies and manipulative reactions and flee. Then again, on the off chance that we remain quiet, they will continue disclosing what is probably going to lead them to come clean.

If you date a girl, tell her your personal story and ask her to keep it a secret. If you trust them with your secret, they will also feel connected to you and share their stories.

Ask a person for help. Don't ask people for help.

Do you need help with your things? Instead of announcing help like 'Can someone fill out this form for me?', You can ask someone for help like 'Hi Robert, can you fill out this form?'.

Although they ask for help from a person, they will most likely accept the request because they will feel responsible if they reject it.

Please frame requests as an option.

People like to have options, and if you want something, you will be more successful if you give them options.

Also, frame your request in a selective answer such as Yes or No. If options are given in the request, the other person will have fewer things to think about and be more likely to make decisions.

So instead of telling someone to finish the job, you should ask, "When can you finish this job? in the afternoon or at night? "

Count to five

The next time you don't want to do something you know you should be doing, tell yourself you're counting to five and then do it. As if you're thinking about skipping the gym, pause for a moment, start counting to five and then get ready for the gym.

It may seem strange, but by counting, we give our brain some time to rationalize the situation and act accordingly, rather than simply making the wrong decision.

Tune in to body language

Connect directly with someone? Just mirror your body language. That's a good trick to get noticed and bond with someone. Yes, but don't overdo it, slightly follow your posture and facial expression without you noticing.

For example, if a seated client loosens their legs and leans slightly while speaking, wait a few seconds and then adopt a similar position.

Chewing gum to reduce anxiety

A study presented at the International Congress of Behavioral Medicine found that chewing gum was associated with increased alertness, decreased anxiety, and better overall multitasking activities.

Chewing gum is also associated with a reduced hormone cortisol level, primarily responsible for anxiety and stress.

So if you are too tense for a meeting, public speaking, or event, bring gum. Chew gum to relieve stress before getting nervous.

- Another great tip is to trick anyone you want to manipulate into doing something you want them to do, but then "just happen" to make it harder for them. But if they come to you and complain about how hard it was, say, "oh, I'm sorry it got so hard. I don't know how it could have happened." And make it look like it wasn't your fault. But before trying this, make sure it's something they can't get out of.

- Take an acting class to help you master your emotions.

- For some people, this comes naturally, so don't try too hard or try to be too obvious.

- Try to show interest in the person and make it seem like they need something. They will be willing to help you.

- Don't try to manipulate someone you know is manipulating people! They can usually see for themselves when you handle them.

- If you are trying to manipulate your parents or friends, choose the weakest link. For example, if you are trying to manipulate your parents into making you do something, go to who you think is most likely to admit it, and make sure you only try when parent number two is out of the room.

- Compliment people and agree with (most) what they say, unless it doesn't make sense and makes you look like an idiot

SIMPLE STRATEGIES FOR READING BODY LANGUAGE QUICKLY

One of the easiest ways to analyze other people is to observe their body language. The way a person holds, moves and even talks to himself can tell you a lot about him. Everyone has a lot of variation in their gestures, and there is no exact way to know what a person is made of. There are still many similar indications among groups of people that can give you a deep understanding of how someone works. It is not easy because you start by becoming aware of your body language. To understand and try to overcome the problem of body language, you must be very aware. In the first book, we walk you through becoming aware of your thoughts and where they may come from. Now is the time to work to become aware of your body.

To find out what makes someone different from others based on their body language, you must first look at yourself and analyze how you hold your body. Some people may be more aware of their movements than their thoughts. Women are likely to become more aware of their bodies and their space, especially due to the patriarchal society in which we grew up. It can still be difficult for anyone to confront the way you hold your body. You may lose concentration when trying to maintain awareness, which will make you too unsure about your own body and movements. This first chapter examines the basic principles of body language and also lays the groundwork for analyzing others. Once you have a better understanding of someone else's body movements, you can likewise comprehend what makes them extraordinary. The more you think about an individual, the better you can build up the best influence technique.

Cultural differences

Every person is different, and sometimes the way a person holds their body has a different meaning than someone standing in the same way. There are many ways that a person's body language differs, so it is important to remember that not everything about a particular exercise is 100% true for everyone. This is particularly imperative to recollect when addressing individuals of various social foundations.

Some cultures practice modesty so that playing can be completely off-limits. Other cultures may be more open to expressing their feelings through their bodies, so it is important to remember the culture when thinking about how someone might use their body.

Study the movements of others

Once you are more aware of body movements and what they can represent, you can begin to study; you can likewise comprehend what makes them extraordinary. The more you think about an individual, the better you can build up the best influence technique. These are some of the small differences that you might see when observing a person's body language. When you study other people and yourself, it is important that you also try to act naturally. It tends to be anything but difficult to become hyper-mindful of your developments, yet realize that you don't need to hold your body in a specific manner.

Not every person is as mindful of body developments as every other person, so don't over-watch your movements at the end of the day. But once you start studying the body movements of others, you will begin to realize how much you can get to know them.

Certain things can make sense after meeting different people. You may notice that one of your friends is quite pretentious about how he behaves or talks to himself. Other friends can show how insecure they are with themselves, even if you thought they were incredibly confident since you met them. Knowing a person's body language and understanding why they are moving in a certain way will help you better understand their essence. This gives you better influence with regards to persuading them. You may want to match your boss's confidence when you make a storage deal.

Knowing his body language can be scary at first, but you will become comfortable with the way he moves over time. Try hanging yourself in front of a mirror to practice getting comfortable with your own body. If you're eating, watching TV, or even lounging in bed, put up a mirror to see how you're holding yourself. Once you understand a stranger's perspective on how they move, you can also see how others move.

Eye contact

Eye contact is one of the best clues you can use to determine what someone is. It is also important that you become aware of your eye contact use, as it provides clues to others about your personality and true nature. Maintaining eye contact is important so that someone knows that you are interested in what they are saying and have your full attention. However, it can also be overused and let people know that you are trying too hard to convince them that you are listening.

Too much eye contact can sometimes be intimidating to others too, so if you notice someone getting nervous about the amount of eye contact you have with them, change it from time to time. Student dilation can be a direct indication that someone is interested in what you are saying. Studies have shown that when someone's pupils start to dilate with whom you make eye contact, they are more interested in what you have to say.

They listen to you with their utmost attention and think deeply about what you say. When someone's pupils dilate while talking to you, you know they are interested in the conversation. Crafty eyes will indicate otherwise. Someone looking you in the eye from side to side is probably trying to convince you that they are listening to you. They are aware that they should try to make eye contact, but they are fully aware of what you are saying. Those with cunning eyes may also lie to you or try to deceive you in some way.

Movements of the mouth

What a person does with their mouth is also very important to understand their personality. Someone with pursed or pursed lips may be trying to focus, or they may also be doing their best to hide a sour face. You can also analyze someone's smile. If the corners of his eyes aren't wrinkled, he can force a smile on you. Someone pretending to smile is not necessarily mean; they may just be thinking about something else, too distracted to give their full attention to what you are saying. Sometimes smiles are also reactions to uncomfortable situations. When monkeys smile, it is not because they are happy, but mainly because they show their teeth to threaten those around them. When they are scared and nervous, they open their mouth wide to show that they have teeth that they can use to hurt.

The same goes for dogs. They only show their teeth when they feel threatened. For humans, this can sometimes be true, but on an unconscious level. Nervous laughter and smiling are just one way a person can ease their tension. You can tell someone is genuinely smiling if they have wrinkles at the corners of their eyes. A person who constantly covers his mouth is also usually nervous. They may bite their lip or finger or put a fist in front of their mouth. Knowing when a person is uncomfortable or nervous can sometimes help convince them.

Assent

The way a person turns and tilts their head can be a subtle movement. Most of the time, others are not so conscious when they shake their heads. The neck and head movements of the person you are talking to can give you a good idea of what they are thinking on a deeper level. Someone who nods their head fairly quickly while listening to you may be anxious and try to get the conversation started as quickly as possible.

They try to set a pace for you to speak faster. They want to let you know they are listening, but you are not speaking fast enough. If someone is doing this to you, try to speak faster to keep their attention. Someone who keeps their head to one side may have a legitimate interest in what you say. They try to turn their ear towards you so they can hear you better, whether they are aware of your movements or not.

They also indicate that they listen to you and want you to keep talking. It's a way for them to get closer to you during the conversation without interfering or interrupting. If someone nods their head too artificially, they may be trying to convince you that they are interested in what you are saying. They may be aware that they need to pay attention, but they may have lost interest.

Trying to keep up, they pretend to nod their heads. They may not understand what you're saying either, so they nod their heads to make you think they're doing it. If you notice that the people around you are artificially nodding their heads, it is worth changing the subject to regain attention or explain yourself better, as they could get confused. Mimicking someone's head movements can be very helpful in using persuasion. A slight nod of the head while listening to them can show you understand what they are saying. It can also show that you are empathetic to them, especially if they seem to be talking about something difficult.

Hands and arms

The way someone uses their hands and arms is another way that body language can be interpreted to help you better understand the people you interact with. Our hands represent a lot about ourselves. They are a way of expressing stories, putting different emphasis on different parts. When someone tells a story, use hand gestures to keep people interested. Think of someone who leads a conversation as someone who leads an orchestra. They raise their hands to keep up with the rhythm and rhythm of those who are listening. A person's hands and arms can also express how open or closed they are.

They can be like the door to someone's body. If they cross forcefully in front of someone's chest, that person may be a bit more closed and not want to engage in too much conversation. Crossed arms don't always mean someone is necessarily closed off. They may also want to rest their arms, so if they hang loosely in front of their chest, they are probably just listening casually. Someone with arms outstretched, perhaps overhead, is likely to be very open and even trying to exert control over a situation. Someone with their hands on their hips may also be trying to assert their strength.

Signs

We all have different questions about the body language that they use as cues. Across cultures, genders, and ages, the different movements a person makes with their body can be conscious or unconscious signals that they give to those around them. The signals allow other people to know bits of information without having to say anything. Someone with folded arms and faded eyes sitting on a couch at a party is sending the signal that he's probably ready to go home for the night.

Someone else on that couch could sit on the edge of your seat, laughing out loud, indicating that they won't be going to bed anytime soon. The signs help the people around the caller know things that they may not express easily with their bodies. Some are very good at picking up other people's signals, and some people have a hard time understanding those around them. When it comes to convincing someone, there are some crucial signs that someone needs to lead a conversation properly.

Start a conversation

The next time you sit quietly in a room with someone else, wait for the conversation to begin to speak. In this way, you can study how they can start a conversation. Most people will give some signals with their bodies that they are going to speak. They can clear their throats, turn their heads, adjust their shirts, or move in their seats. Usually, there is something, however minor, that someone does right before starting a conversation. When it is your turn to start a conversation, pay attention to what you are doing before you start speaking.

Don't start with "eh" or "eh." This way, the other person will know immediately that you are not sure what to say. Try to start a conversation without doing anything. See if you can start talking without clearing your throat, moving your head, or doing anything else. Study how the others response. They may be surprised or puzzled that one of you started talking. Starting a conversation, especially one intended to convince another, is important in laying the groundwork for your argument. No one will want to give their full attention to someone who is struggling to get started. When you're nervous and jump over your words, it becomes much more challenging to keep up.

Leading the conversation

Once the conversation has started, it can be tricky to keep the right amount going back and forth. You would prefer not to be excessively forceful, yet you additionally don't need them to blabber and not have the opportunity to score your focuses.

If you feel like the other person is not allowing you to speak enough, there are obvious phrases you can use to express your opinion. You could try saying something like, "can I just say ..." "can I have a chat?" or "I'm listening, but can I say something very quickly?" This can be difficult to say in some situations, and some people will even find it rude if you make a big interjection. Maybe the best thing you can do is use your body to shift focus. Put your hands on your hips or bow your head, so the other person knows you have something to say.

Try to lean in to let them know that you want to take over their current conversation. Leading the conversation can be tricky because no one wants to hear someone interrupt them. It is still important that it is your turn to speak. There are ways you can practice leading conversations so you can lead the right way when it comes time to have an important belief. The next time you want to say something, don't do it. Instead, let the other person continue talking and intervene later.

Sometimes we are so afraid to say our part that we get distracted from the actual conversation and invalidate any arguments we have against the person we interrupt. An alternative way to practice directing the conversation is to say something the next time you want to say something. If you have something to say but prefer to keep your mouth shut, force yourself to say whatever you want. These two practice methods provide you with two alternative perspectives on how to carry on a conversation that you would not otherwise have.

How your body language affects you

Believe it or not, the way you use your body can also directly affect how it works. There are ways that you can use to improve your thinking and memory capacity simply by the way you use your hands and arms. Not only are there physical differences in the way you use your body, but you will also be affected by the way others perceive you. If you are constantly closed and always cross your arms, there are probably many people who are not open or do not speak to you because they assume that you have no interest in a conversation. If you are always very open with your body, exercise self-confidence, and stand tall, others may feel intimidated by you. You may have no intention of shutting up or intimidating others, but your body can show it in a way that your mouth cannot. It can be difficult to notice your body movements, but you can change how someone else thinks of you once you do.

Some people may have very conscious minds, but they may hate their bodies. They can then silence others by trying to hide their bodies, making others think they are critical. Sometimes a person is only trying to cover her body and not herself. You would be surprised how much confidence you can feel by changing the way you hold your body. People can still see how you look even if you keep your arms crossed. You may think that you are changing the perception that other people have of you, but you remain closed in reality. There are other ways that your body language can affect you mentally.

Open your mind

Someone who opens their arms while speaking will begin to let others know that they have a much more open mind. Standing with your arms open or just hanging relaxed by your side is letting those around you know that you are confident and willing to talk to them about different things. While having your arms open is a signal to others, it is also a signal to your brain. Studies show that by standing with arms wide open and verses crossed. You will come up with new ideas that you would not do if you crossed your arms. The same goes for the rest of your body. The more open you are with your movements, the more you allow your brain to have different ideas.

Improve your memory

Those who speak with their hands also tend to have better memories than those who don't. Using your hands can place physical memories in your brain for ideas and thoughts you might discuss. If you imitate numbers or shapes when talking about different ideas, especially in a business setting, not only will you remember what you are discussing, but the people around you will find your story most memorable. Using your hands to speak while telling a story can also help you remember the things you've been through. You stimulate your brain to keep thinking, and by keeping your arms open, as we mentioned in the previous section, you will open your brain to new thoughts and feelings that you might not have had if you folded your arms closed.

The strength of your body

 Our bodies have a lot of strength, and not just how much we can lift or carry. Physical strength is important, but even the weakest people can control a room with just body movements. At this point in the book, you should have a basic understanding of what someone's body language could mean. We cannot go into all the specific details of what a person's physical actions might convey, but the framework for analyzing those movements is there. Once you understand how someone else could use their body to convince others, you can start working on your persuasiveness.

There are many ways people can use their bodies to convince others to do what they want, but it won't always work for everyone. Some people respond to sexual persuasion, while others resist the thought. Some people respond to a physical threat from those who seem stronger than they are, but others may be ready for battle. There are numerous ways you can utilize your body to convince others without intimidating them sexually or physically. Keeping your body open and visible is crucial so that others know that they can trust you.

Try to make sure you remove the physical barriers that can keep you separate from the person you are talking to. Stand around a chair or table that prevents you from fully connecting with the person you are trying to talk to. This also shows that you are confident and interested in expressing your opinion while listening to what the other person has to say. By analyzing others' movements, you can also find out what you can do to increase your self-confidence. Study certain celebrities and see how they behave in different settings. Everyone has their moves, but by mimicking others, you can still find your grip when it comes to an overall convincing stance.

Smiling is important

Our smile is one of the most powerful tools that we have been given. You can change any circumstance from awful to great by lifting the edges of your mouth. A few people feel that they are useless on the off chance that they don't have straight teeth or a splendid white grin. Indeed, even the individuals who don't have the entirety of their teeth can have many prettier grins than somebody who has burned through thousands of dental work. A grin isn't just about the teeth it shows.

It is a way of involving another person. Studies have shown that most people will smile if someone smiles at them first. When they smile, they will generally be in a better mood. It may seem strange, but simply smiling can lift a person's spirits. Smile the next time you're feeling particularly down. It sounds so crazy, but it could work. Smile over and over again, and while it may not change your mood, it will help cheer you up, at least temporarily.

VERBAL SIGNS

While there are many things a person can say with their body, they can say many more things with their mouth. There are a seemingly infinite number of languages available, as each specific language has many subparts. Think about how many different accents there can be in New York City alone. As we continue to develop and mix different cultures and languages, they will only develop further. It's hard enough to keep track of what we already know, but there are ways to grasp others' meaning without having to memorize every word in the dictionary. Just because someone says a certain word doesn't mean they mean what they say. How many times have you said it was "okay" when you wanted to blow your mind?

We always say what we don't mean because it is not always easy to express our thoughts and feelings in words. Many people transfer their frustration or sadness to other people when they don't mean what they say. Knowing why people say what they do can be one of the most difficult codes to crack. It is not always necessary to know exactly what someone is trying to say to understand what they are trying to say. You can capture a person's intention by listening to how they speak and mixing that with their body language.

It's important to read someone's mood, so you don't say the wrong thing or say something that could change the conversation's direction. The next time you find something on TV in a different language than you can speak, try watching it without subtitles. You will be surprised that you understand part of the story. Don't look at what they say; look at how they say it. Is there pain in your eyes? Do they look happy or sad? If you don't understand what someone is saying, perhaps because the room is noisy or speaking quietly, try looking them in the eye. You may have a better idea of what they are saying than just looking at the words trying to put your mouths together.

There are certain specific tips that a person can give when trying to lead a conversation. If you are trying to convince someone, you can use various keywords to help you lead the conversation. Some people rely too much on the actual words someone says when they should try to hear their message. It may seem not easy to figure out what someone else is saying, but it is possible. Think of your pets. You can tell if your dog is sad, sleepy, hungry, or playful, but you do not have real conversations with him. Sometimes you can analyze what someone says better by finding out what sounds they make, rather than analyzing every word. Emphasize the signals.

Emphasize the signals

When you're trying to convince someone, you want a good, ready-made argument to build your case. You may want to include some emphatic cues when you speak. These phrases can be difficult to incorporate in nature, but it's good to practice so that you can become a better persuader

"This is important," "you need to know," "let me explain" are phrases that capture the attention of the person you are talking to. You may notice emphatic instructions from other people after reading this section. You should listen to and use phrases in your speech that seem to emphasize an important part of a conversation.

Sometimes these emphasis attributes aren't even actual sentences. They can only be verbal cues that something is important, such as someone raising their voice when talking about an important part of their speech. They can also repeat or pause the word multiple times so that the listener can record what you just said. It is important to understand accented signals to understand better what may be important to an individual. Hearing what they emphasize will also help you formulate your thoughts and arguments about the things that are important to them.

Organizational signs

"First, second, third," "to summarize," "the subject is," are all expressions that can be considered organizational clues. These cues help a person indicate that they are trying to collect their thoughts, again perhaps by emphasizing the

The things that matter most.

Organizational cues are important for you to use in your belief arguments so that people are on your side. You want them to know that you are listening to what they have to say and they should listen to you. You are trying to formulate a plan based on your thoughts and opinions, not just a specific individual's words.

Organizational cues allow the speaker to emphasize what is important, while at the same time maintaining clear thinking and direct focus. Organizational signs cannot be expressions either. It could just be someone who clears their throat, redirects the conversation to an earlier topic, or stops so everyone can organize their thoughts.

Watch your launch

The tone is an important key when trying to steer the conversation in their favor. The tone is the level of your voice and the overall quality of the sound. Someone with a deep tone may have a lower tone, while someone with a high tone can alert listeners. Not everyone can avoid the natural tone of their voice. Some people with extremely low voices are difficult to hear, and some people have naturally shrill voices that seem to be annoying everyone around them.

While your natural tone can't always be controlled, it can at least help to focus that tone into a more productive tone to keep your listeners engaged with what you have to say. Many of us let our pitch get too high and whiny when trying to keep our dictation sharp in a professional setting. If you feel like your voice is getting high and sharp, don't be afraid to stop, clear your throat, and start over. The people around you will probably be grateful that you adjust your pitch for their listening pleasure.

Be careful not to raise the end of your voice while speaking. Many people, especially when talking on the phone, tend to end their words as if they ask a question. This type of speech is also common among those who may be giving a speech. They say a sentence very clearly with dictation, but they also end the sentence with a high tone as if they are asking a question. This is something to avoid to keep your listeners' attention.

It is important to find your optimal shade. Some people have very soft voices that are difficult to hear. If so, it is important to practice speaking when necessary. Someone who tends to speak loudly should try to speak quietly as often as possible to balance their tone. The best way to practice is alone and when you record what you say. You don't want to over-analyze the way you speak, but practice always helps, especially for those who have trouble speaking.

It is also important to have a safe speech so that others know they can hear it. Someone who always speaks shyly or as if asking a question will let those around them know that what they have to say is not interesting. The best way to get others to pay attention is to make sure you speak confidently.

Listen to others

Talking about yourself can evoke the same good feelings as money and food. People talk about themselves more than they like to listen to other people who talk about themselves for the most part. While it may seem selfish, most people indeed prefer to talk about themselves. This means that when talking to other people, you should avoid talking too much about yourself.

You don't want the whole conversation to be about other people, but no one will pay attention if you're only talking about yourself. Giving advice can also be helpful, but people generally don't get in touch with those who give too much advice, especially when they aren't asked for it.

Listening to other people can even be a challenge for some. It can be hard not to let your mind wander, especially if the other person talks too much about themselves. Some people will find that they generally form their next thought while the other person is speaking, rather than listening to them. If you find your mind wandering when speaking, redirect your thoughts back to their words. Don't just listen to what they say. See how they say it. Hear their voice and look them in the eye. People will notice if you listen to them. Even if they are not adept at body language, they will feel that you are not fully engaged either.

Don't emphasize just listening to others. Have a conversation about them too.

You will find that people generally like to answer questions about themselves. This is often a technique that you find with many salespeople. They will ask you where you bought your shirt or if you had a decent day. This is to get the individual considering themselves and normally wind up being more open with the sales rep.

People don't like to be corrected. While it can sometimes be difficult to avoid, most people don't want to be bothered by being told they were wrong. Most people will respect you a lot more if you let them speak instead of proving them wrong. This is critical to recollect, particularly with regards to persuading and examining others.

Talk about "us", not "you". If you are trying to make suggestions, perhaps to a colleague or friend on how to improve your lifestyle, use "we". Don't say "you should try to get up earlier on the weekend" but rather "we should get up early on Sunday and go for a walk together!" People will react much better to recommendations if you get included.

Apologize

It can be not easy to apologize, especially to those with a high degree of pride, but it is important to earn the respect of those around you. If you apologize for being late instead of giving every possible explanation, most will respond much better than if you tried to look better with apologies.

They also like to see humility and that you are not afraid to express yourself. "I'm sorry I didn't reply to your text, I just had a really bad day," It's usually very forgiving rather than when you just impressed him.

However, don't be too embarrassed. It can make others not trust you. Sometimes we tend to apologize for things we couldn't control, trying to make ourselves look better. We will say, "I'm sorry the movie was so bad!" Going out after a movie night, even though we had no control over the production. This is nice at times, and it certainly shows humility and vulnerability to those around you. But too much of this can also make you dishonest to other people.

If you need to apologize after each easily overlooked detail you state, why would anyone listen to you in the first place? The next time you feel the need to apologize for something you can't control, try saying thank you. After a long talk with a friend, don't say, "I'm sorry you had to listen to me!" Instead, try something like, "Thanks for listening so well. Happy to have a companion like you! "Individuals will, by and large, react significantly more emphatically to a thankful individual than somebody who consistently discredits himself. You will find that you will treat yourself much better on the off chance that you additionally cling to this strategy for a statement of regret."

PERSUASION

Belief is defined as the process by which a communicator tries to influence other people to change their behavior or attitude towards a problem by transmitting a message. The main elements of faith are: Persuasion is symbolic where the communicator has to use words, sounds, images and others.

Persuasion is a deliberate attempt to change a person's beliefs or opinions.

Self-confidence is necessary because people must have the freedom to choose. The method by which the message is transmitted can be done in various ways, such as verbal and non-verbal, through radio, the Internet, or direct communication.

However, not all communication types can convince people, as it can be for entertainment or to provide information. Influence can be utilized to control individuals, and in this way, attempting to persuade others can be viewed as disgusting conduct. When analyzed as a process, belief can be distinguished from communication as a stimulus to the associated behavioral changes resulting from the effector response.

Here we will see the steps that a person goes through when persuaded. First, there is the presence of communication where the recipient will pay attention to the content presented. Then you will try to understand the content of the communication as a whole, including trying to understand what the speaker is trying to say. This also includes trying to understand the conclusion suggested by the speaker, as well as any evidence.

That can be provided to support the conclusion. Persuasion occurs only when the individual finally accepts or agrees with the given point and must maintain this interest long enough to act accordingly. The main purpose of persuasion is to get the individual or group of people to adopt a new attitude.

Examples include changing a brand of breakfast cereal because new information is presented to them or when someone changes their religious beliefs.

Some theorists insist that there is a difference between education and persuasion. While belief and education are similar in that they provide new information through communication, they are not always the same. Repeated communication can affect learning, showing that it has a compelling impact on people at some point. Likewise, there are principles in verbal communication that are also widely used by successful persuaders.

One way to look at this is to repeatedly use informational TV ads as a way of trying to convince consumers to make an informed behavior change, like using a different brand of toothpaste, because you now think it's healthier. For them. How someone responds to a persuasive message depends, of course, on the message itself and the way a person perceives or interprets it. According to perception theorists, belief is the process by which a person's perception or attitude is changed. There is additional proof that the achievement of influence relies upon an individual's inclinations, which are similarly as significant as the message.

When talking about persuasion, it is also important to note that persuasion involves finding a compromise between conflicting forces some theorists say. These forces include existing attitudes and prejudices, individual desires, social pressures, and new information. This model of conflict resolution is also known as balance, congruence, or consistency. It's about how people engage their existing strengths and tune them into their existing attitudes.

According to some theorists, belief is related to an intellectual aspect, while it is related to emotional considerations in others.

The top 4 ways persuasion differs today from how it was in the past:

1. People are more exposed to compelling messages daily than ever. To prove it, try to remember the number of ads you see each day. Studies show that an average American is exposed to between 300 and 3,000 ads per day.

2. Compelling communication through the Internet, radio and television is faster.

3. You can make money with persuasion. Many companies are in the market for persuasion purposes only, including public relations firms, advertising agencies, and marketing firms.

Modern persuasion methods are more subtle.

Attribution theory

The attribution theory of persuasion looks at how people attempt to describe others' actions through situational or dispositional attribution. Situational attribution, also called external attribution, attempts to explain the behavior of other people in the context of their environment and surroundings. Situational attribution primarily involves aspects of an individual's environment that are beyond his or her control. An example of situational attribution would be to explain that a person's behavior is due to the family environment in which they grew up, rather than indicating that it is just their choice of actions.

On the other hand, dispositional attribution of internal attribution tries to explain a person's behavior by observing their traits, dispositions, motives, and abilities. It occurs when people do certain things because it is easier for them than doing the right thing for those around them.

Fundamental attribution is when people incorrectly attribute an achievement or deficiency based on external and internal factors, but the opposite occurs. By default, people tend to make dispositional attributions when trying to understand a person's behavior when, in fact, they should grant situational attributions. This is especially the case if we don't know someone very well, so we don't have enough information about their situation.

When we try to convince other people to do things for us or even to like us, we tend to explain positive actions with character traits. However, when we try to explain our negative behavior, we tend to use situational attribution.

Conditioning theories

Conditioning is one of the most important concepts in persuasion. The concept of conditioning has to do with encouraging someone to do something for themselves rather than directing them to do something, like the concept of obedience.

Conditioning is widely used in the advertising industry, where brands try to evoke positive feelings with their brand or logo. For this reason, brands turn to ads that encourage people to laugh, feel sentimental, or use upbeat music and images. Once these commercials are done, they display the brand's logo to connect positive emotion with their product.

Conditioning is used because emotions affect the way people perceive products or brands. People tend to shop because it makes them feel good. The basis of emotion is an important factor in the purchase. Ads are repeated because they hope that by repeating the message multiple times, the viewer is more likely to buy the product to connect with a positive emotion or experience.

Theory of cognitive dissonance

Leon Festinger first proposed the theory of cognitive dissonance in 1956. According to this theory, people, by nature, always strive for mental coherence. All of our thoughts, attitudes, and beliefs may be unrelated, consistent, or at odds. Also, our thoughts, attitudes and beliefs cannot be related to our behavior. When we feel that there is inconsistency in our thoughts and actions, we feel uncomfortable. An excellent example of cognitive dissonance is a person who practices an unhealthy lifestyle, knowing that it is bad for them.

According to Festinger, we are motivated to decrease dissonance until we feel the harmony between our thoughts and behavior. It suggests that there are four ways people try to reduce dissonance: 1. Reduce the importance of cognition 2. Change your mind about one or more aspects of behavior 3. Reassess the cost/reward ratio

4. Increase the overlap between thinking and behavior In the situation of the person who leads an unhealthy lifestyle, you can make changes to adapt and become healthier, reduce the importance of a healthy lifestyle, convince yourself that it is not. Poses a risk or concludes that healthier lifestyle rewards outweigh the benefits of an unhealthy lifestyle.

Theory of social judgment

Social judgment theory suggests that people's natural reaction is to find a way to sort the information in their heads when presented with a compelling idea. The information is first evaluated and compared to the person's current beliefs, also known as the anchor point or initial latitude.

These latitudes have different levels: we tend to assess whether it falls within the range of avoidance, acceptance, rejection or indifference. The involvement of one's ego plays a very important role in determining where the idea falls. If the idea with which we are trying to be persuaded has to do with how we see ourselves or something that matters to us, the margin of maneuver of non-commitment and acceptance is usually much smaller. In comparison, the margin of rejection would be less. The anchor point is a person's center of acceptance, and it is when someone takes a position that it is most acceptable to them.

When an audience obtains information, they tend to distort the information first to fit their unique latitudes. When you are within a person's acceptance rate, they will integrate the information and probably consider it closer to their anchor point, even though there may still be a great distance. Therefore, when trying to convince someone, it is important to know your audience's different latitudes. The best way to be successful would be to use compelling information that is almost acceptable to your audience if you want to change your anchor point. When people repeatedly suggest an idea, people tend to adjust their anchor points gradually. But if you propose ideas that fall within the area of rejection and their avoidance attitude, it will not result in a change in actions or beliefs.

Inoculation theory

The inoculation theory is often observed in comparative types of advertisements. The inoculation theory suggests that one party has a weak argument whose credibility can be crushed by the public, so the other party's best argument will follow.

Narrative transport theory

Narrative transport theory claims that people's attitudes can change when they get lost in a story. Try to explain the compelling effect of stories on individuals as they can experience narrative transport when different conditions are met. Also, the story's transport occurs when the listener wants to enter another world because the story evokes certain feelings, especially empathy for the characters in the story.

Persuasion methods

There are many different persuasion methods, also known as persuasion strategies or persuasion tactics.

1. The use of force is about making demands. It can be perceived as a threat because the persuader offers no options, and the public has no choice but to follow directions.

2. Robert Cialdini suggested six weapons of influence that are also used in persuasion. These are:

to. Reciprocity: Cialdini's principle of reciprocity states that we are naturally inclined to return the favor when someone gives us something. The act of reciprocity evokes a sense of obligation in people, which is often considered compelling. The principle of reciprocity is also powerful because people feel compelled to give back. People have a natural tendency to dislike people who don't do a favor or offer payment when they receive something for free. This is why reciprocity is a common social standard for many cultures around the world.

Yes. Commitment and Consistency: Consistency is considered one of the most important aspects of persuasion. A highly valued virtue in many cultures results in a healthy approach to life and offers people a shortcut to modern life complications.

When we experience consistency, it is easier for us to process information and make informed decisions. People tend to be more committed to their actions when they explain them orally or in writing. That is why written commitments are widely used; Not only do they serve as strong evidence, but the written ideas seem more psychologically concrete.

Commitment is a powerful persuasion tool because if you can convince someone to commit to something, they are more likely to persuade.

Themselves and, ultimately, give themselves and other reasons to support their action.

C. Social Proof: By nature, we are easily influenced by the people around us. Normally, we want to do what others do. People often base their beliefs on what they see happening in their environment. In this sense, "crowd power" is effective because we always want to know what other people around us are doing. Most people, unknowingly, are so obsessed with what other people do and how they act. However, social proof is only powerful when people feel unsure of themselves or when there are similarities within a situation. People are more likely to adjust to what other people do when the situation is unclear, as there are many options. We are also more likely to change when the people around us are like us.

Re. Taste: The concept of this weapon of influence is simple: people say yes to people they like. Two factors affect a person's likeability. The first states that physical attractiveness plays a role because people who are more attractive to other people can easily convince others. When other people find you physically attractive, it's easier to get them to do what you want. The second liking factor is resemblance: if people like you, they are more likely to say yes to what you want. It is more natural for people to change their opinions and beliefs for the people they like; in fact, we don't usually think about it because it happens more naturally.

Me. Authority: People are more likely to listen to someone if they think they are an expert on a topic. When we find someone who is knowledgeable and trustworthy, we tend to listen to them more. It will be easier to convince people if they think you have both since you already did half the work.

F. Scarcity: The concept of scarcity in persuasion is often underestimated but argued

That when a product has limited availability, it becomes more valuable. Cialdini says that people want more than they cannot have. However, when using scarcity in persuasion, it is important to remember the context. Scarcity is only effective in certain contexts. If you want people to believe that a product is scarce, you must be clear about what this product has and what others do not.

3. Machiavellianism: Refers to the use of deception and manipulation to gain power.

Aristotle also described three ways to change a person's opinion:

1. Ethos: refers to trust and how much integrity is perceived by the speaker. It would help if you had a good reputation to be trusted. It consists of 3 other elements:

to. Reputation: A person's reputation depends on his past and what other people say about him. If someone wants to use their reputation for persuasion, they must show a glorious past and remind other people of their successes.

Yes. Character: According to Aristotle, the character aspect of the ethos presents people as three-dimensional and subject to the same defects. People are subject to the same kinds of problems as other people. Show a virtuous person who will maintain good values.

C. Credibility: This depends on a person's experience and how they portray themselves. But for people to believe you, you must first show that you believe in yourself. It would help if you also position yourself as an expert on the subject you want to convince people. As you speak, show that you can address any arguments you come across. You can also do things to position yourself as a leader when speaking, such as eye contact and hand gestures.

2. Pathos: Pathos appeals to the emotions of a person where the main objective is

Arouse their interest or enthusiasm. One of the most effective ways to arouse someone's emotions is by appealing to their values. Ethos is how people can show their values, like talking about stories where innocent people have been harmed. It is a way of showing other people what is important to them and putting other people in front of you. Another way is to work with the goals of the listener or challenge their beliefs. This is where the importance of language comes into play, as the right words can significantly affect people's emotions.

Logos - focuses on rational explanation and cool logic, along with evidence. Empirical evidence is a form of logos necessary for scientific evidence. Providing evidence is difficult to deny and can be presented in statistics, experience, and photographs. A first-hand experience is a powerful form of evidence. The reason is another form of a logo that makes use of rational points as accepted truths and theories. If there is no evidence, and efficient convict can still use reason to prove his position. An effective way to use reasoning is to combine cause and effect.

THE SUBTLE DIFFERENCE BETWEEN PERSUASION AND MANIPULATION

Calling somebody manipulative is an analysis of that individual's character. Saying that you have been controlled is an objection of misuse. Control is temperamental, best case scenario and out and out corrupt even from a pessimistic standpoint. Be that as it may, why would that be? Shouldn't something be said about control? Individuals continually impact each other from various perspectives. Yet, what recognizes control from different impacts, and what makes it unethical?

We are continually liable to endeavors at control. Here are a few models. There is "gaslighting," which means that someone is encouraged to question their judgment and, instead, to trust the manipulator's advice. Guilt makes a person feel too guilty for not doing what the manipulator wants him to do. Charm offensives and peer pressure make a person so preoccupied with the manipulator's approval that he will do whatever the manipulator wants.

Then there is a more direct manipulation; perhaps the best-known example of this is when Iago manipulates Othello to arouse suspicions about Desdemona's fidelity, plays on his insecurities to make him jealous and provokes a rage that leads Othello to kill his lover. All of these examples of manipulation share a sense of immortality. What do they have in common?

Perhaps manipulation is wrong because it hurts the person being manipulated. Handling certainly often hurts. If successful, manipulative cigarette ads contribute to illness and death; Manipulative phishing and other scams facilitate identity theft and other forms of fraud; manipulative social tactics can encourage abuse or unhealthy relationships. Political manipulation can provoke divisions and weaken democracy. But manipulation is not always harmful.

Suppose Amy has just left an abusive but loyal partner, but she is tempted to get back with him in a moment of weakness. Now imagine Amy's friends using the same techniques that Iago used on Othello. They manipulate Amy into believing (falsely) and being enraged that her ex-partner was abusive and unfaithful. On the off chance that this control forestalls Amy from accommodating, she may be in an ideal situation than she would have been if her companions hadn't controlled her. Be that as it may, it might at present appear to be ethically problematic to many. Instinctively, it would have been ethically better for her companions to utilize non-manipulative intends to help Amy evade a backslide. Something remains ethically dubious about control, regardless of whether it helps instead of mischief the individual being controlled. Like this, harm can't be the purpose behind ill-advised dealing with.

Maybe control isn't right since it includes methods that are naturally indecent ways. This thought may be especially appealing to those inspired by Immanuel Kant's idea that morality requires that we treat each other as rational beings rather than mere objects. Perhaps the only correct way to influence other rational beings' behavior is through rational persuasion, and therefore any influence other than rational persuasion is morally inappropriate. However, this answer is also short for all its appeal, as it would condemn many forms of morally benign influence.

Much of Iago's manipulation, for example, appeals to Othello's emotions. But emotional calls aren't always manipulative. Moral belief often appeals to empathy or tries to convey how you would feel if others did what you do to you. Likewise, it doesn't seem like manipulation to scare someone over something really dangerous, feel guilty about something truly immoral, or feel a reasonable level of confidence in someone's true capabilities. Even invitations to question someone's judgment may not be manipulative in situations where, perhaps, due to intoxication or strong emotions, there is a good reason to do so. Not all forms of non-rational influence appear to be manipulative.

So it seems that whether an influence is manipulative depends on how it is utilized. Iago's activities are manipulative and wrong since they intend to cause Othello to think and feel inappropriately. Iago realizes that Othello has no motivation to be envious; however, it makes him desirous. This is the passionate simple to the trickiness that Iago additionally rehearses when fixing things (for instance, the tissue that tumbled) to fool Othello into shaping convictions that Iago knows to be bogus. Manipulative gaslighting occurs when the manipulator deceives another and distrusts what the manipulator recognizes as good judgment.

On the other hand, advising an angry friend not to make quick judgments before cooling down is not an act of manipulation, if you know that your friend's judgment is truly temporarily inadequate. When a scammer tries to make you feel empathy for a non-existent Nigerian prince, they act manipulatively because they know it would be wrong to empathize with someone who does not exist. But a sincere call for empathy for real people suffering from excessive misery is a moral conviction instead of control. At the point when a damaging accomplice attempts to make you liable because you speculate him of the betrayal he dedicated, he acts manipulatively because he is attempting to bring about lost blame. However, when a companion causes you to feel suitable blame for forsaking him in his scarcity period, he doesn't appear to be manipulative.

What makes an impact manipulative and what makes it wrong is the equivalent: the controller attempts to get somebody to manage what the controller himself sees as an improper conviction, feeling, or another perspective. Along these lines, control resembles lying. What says something a falsehood and what makes it ethically wrong is the equivalent: that the speaker is attempting to persuade somebody.

The manipulator may do that, but may also try to make you feel an inappropriate emotion (or inappropriately strong or weak), give too much importance to the wrong things (for example, someone else's approval), or abuse something. You doubt (for example, your judgment) that there is no good reason to doubt. The distinction between manipulative and non-manipulative influence depends on whether the influencer is trying to get someone to make a mistake in what they think, feel, doubt, or pay regard for.

It is endemic to the human condition that we impact each other from numerous points of view other than unadulterated discerning conviction. Once in a while, these impacts improve the other individual's dynamic circumstance by causing them to believe, doubt, feel, or pay attention to the right things; sometimes, they reduce decision making by making you believe, doubt, feel or pay attention to the wrong things. But manipulation involves the deliberate use of such influences to hinder one's ability to make the right decision; that is the fundamental indecency of control.

This contemplating control reveals to us something about how to remember it. It's tempting to think of manipulation as some influence. But as we have seen, the types of influences that can be used to manipulate can also be used non-manipulatively. Identifying manipulation is not about what kind of influence is used, but whether the influence is used to put the other in a better or worse position to make a decision. So, if we want to recognize manipulation, we should not look at the form of influence, but rather the intention of the person using it. The purpose is to lower another's decision-making situation, which is both the essence and the essential immorality of manipulation.

HOW TO ANALYZE PEOPLE

Several skills are essential in analyzing people. The first and perhaps most important skill is having an understanding of human nature and normal human behavior. If you do not have a sense of how humans behave under normal circumstances or what motivates most people, you are unlikely to interpret others' actions and intentions correctly. Just as a judge relies on their sense of how people typically behave and what motivates them in their judgments, so too must you develop an understanding of the typical spectrum of human behavior to analyze someone properly.

Of course, human beings can behave in highly original ways, which makes the process of analyzing them difficult at times. Although human beings frequently behave in typically human ways – like being jealous at the success of others, or envious of a colleague who just married a beautiful wife – sometimes people can surprise you. Indeed, some people never feel jealous or envious of others. Most poor people do not steal even though they may need this because it is not part of their character. Frequently the most significant, most flamboyant thief is the person who already has all that they need.

That being said, to analyze people, you are going to have to start with knowing how humans are generally. This includes understanding the spectrum of human emotion, the behaviors linked to these emotions, and the things that motivate people to do this. Everyone wears a mask, which means that sometimes the intentions of others are not always clear. But even with this mask, people can reveal their emotional state to you, the things that make them happy, and the things that make them sad.

We all wear a mask, but perhaps only FBI agents are so skilled that they never give you some clue. A spontaneous laugh, a twinkle in the eye, a giddy tapping of the foot: these are unconscious signs that men and women give of how they feel. Analyzing men and women appropriately will require taking a basic understanding of human behavior and using it to interpret the things that people say and do.

Non-verbal Communication

Non-verbal communication refers to the little clues that others give us that convey essential information to us outside of language. Human beings are social animals, which means that we evolved in settings where we were generally close to one another rather than alone. For this reason, we developed the ability to perceive and interpret the signals that others send to indicate their emotional state, thoughts, and motivations.

It is easy to pay attention to words when we are attempting to analyze others. Still, because language is not always an accurate indication of how people feel, it is essential to also pay attention to the non-verbal cues that others send. These cues can include facial expression, body distance, and the position of hands, quick movements of the hands or the feet, and the like. These non-verbal cues are not specific to human beings. Non-human primates are excellent examples of how animal societies can be built without speech. From bearing of teeth to the position of the tail, apes have a language comprised entirely of non-verbal cues.

Differentiating Fake from Real Emotion

Analyzing others accurately will require developing the ability to distinguish exact sentiment from a false one. Human beings know that others are observing and interpreting them, at least the intelligent ones do, so they have become adept at hiding their feelings. A typical example of this is someone who smiles even though they are not happy, but this hiding of emotion can mean appearing to be angry when one is really hurt or vulnerable. Human beings wear masks to protect themselves, as you must if you plan on defending yourself from practitioners of dark psychology. But protecting yourself also means analyzing people appropriately, and this means determining which emotions are real and which are not.

The practitioner of dark psychological tactics perceives you as prey, so they are paying very close attention to your words, actions, non-verbal cues: virtually anything that indicates what's going on inside. You may put a wall to make your emotions more difficult for the predator to access, but you will most likely say or do something to reveal the truth. This is just as true of the predator as it is of you, the prey. They can put on a façade of smiles and pleasantries, but sometimes all it takes is one fierce look to reveal that their intentions are not so friendly.

We see this all the time in films and television shows. The new neighbor seems nice, but when your back is turned, the camera shot reveals their subtle change in expression. They are not so neighborly. Their goal is to steal your husband and wreak havoc in your life (in the case of the standard Lifetime Original Movie). To protect yourself, you need to use your understanding of human nature and your ability to analyze it to figure out what is going on. Is there a discrepancy between the surface emotion and the events taking place? Perhaps the other person is smiling, but you heard that they lost their house and are short of funds. Would most people be so giddy in this situation?

An essential part of distinguishing real from fake emotion is deciding whether the surface or "fake" feeling makes sense, given what you know. Also, there is a useful expression here. "When people show you who they are, believe them." Human beings are good at being emotionally aware by dint of being so communal. A person can hide what they feel, but it may only take a brief glimmer of real emotion for you to establish the rule of what is real in this person and what is not. When the other person drops their mask for a second, make a note of what the real person beneath looks like.

Tips to Identify a Liar

Anyone who has spent time around a pathological liar knows that there are little tricks that can be used to tell when fibbing. Pathological liars are often highly friendly people who love to talk and always have something to say. It is this still having something to say that gets them into trouble. If you are suspicious that the person you are speaking to is a pathological liar, pay attention to the factual aspects of the things they say. This will become natural in time as you become aware the person is lying. You will make a mental note about facts like a specific monetary amount of something, a date, or the name of a restaurant because you know these things may potentially be false.

Paying close attention to the details is the first step in identifying a liar, and the second is knowing when to face the liar with the facts. It may not be a good idea to confront them pointedly as you may decide, it is better that they did not know that you are onto them. If they said they went to a particular restaurant, ask them what they had to eat—baked chicken and mixed vegetable stir fry. Later or the next day, asks them how the steak was. If they say, it was beautiful when you have caught them. They did not go to the restaurant at all. A pathological liar tells so many lies that they cannot keep track of them.

EMOTIONAL MANIPULATION

Manipulation is another form of mind control that can be used in various ways to determine how the individual will think. In this manual, manipulation refers to psychological manipulation. This is a type of social influence that works around the behavior or perception of others. This is done with the help of abusive, deceptive and dishonest tactics. This form of mind control is used to further the interests of the manipulator, often with others' costs.

The methods used are often considered misleading,

cunning, insulting and exploitative. Many people will recognize when they are being manipulated or when other people around them are being manipulated, but they do not recognize this as a mindset.

Check. This can often be a difficult way to avoid mind control, as manipulation often takes place between the subject and someone they know well.

Requirement for Successful Handling

Successful psychological manipulation mainly includes:

- Manipulative who hides aggressive intentions and behaviors

- Manipulate who knows the psychological vulnerabilities of the victim to determine which tactics may be most effective.

- Manipulator with a sufficient degree of cruelty so as not to have difficulty harming the victim if necessary.

As a result, the manipulation is likely to be hidden (relational aggressive or passive-aggressive).

How manipulators control their victims

- **positive reinforcement** - includes praise, superficial charm, superficial sympathy (crocodile tears), excessive apologies; money, approval, gifts; attention, facial expressions such as a forced laugh or smile; public recognition

- **Negative reinforcement:** includes whining, yelling, silent treatment, intimidation, threats, swearing, emotional blackmail, blame trap, sulking, crying, and playing the victim.

- **Intermittent or Partial Reinforcement:** Partial or intermittent negative reinforcement can create an effective climate of fear and doubt, as in terrorist attacks. Partial or intermittent positive reinforcement can encourage the victim to persevere; for example, in most gambling forms, the player occasionally wins, but generally still loses money.

punishment

Traumatic one-time learning uses verbal abuse, explosive anger, or other intimidating behavior to establish dominance or superiority; even an incident of such behavior can condition or train victims not to annoy, confront or contradict the handler.

Signs of tampering

Shirk responsibility

Someone who wants to manipulate you will often avoid taking responsibility for their actions. Instead of doing that, they will change your own words to make you the "bad" or guilty person in the relationship. Instead of taking ownership of a situation and actions, the manipulator will try to twist the situation so that something you did leads to the problem.

Denying previous promises

Someone who manipulates you may promise to do something or give confirmation when asked, but they will never do what they said. However, bringing this up will point it out again. They will swear that you did not understand what they said and that they are forgetful or ridiculous. This can lead you to question yourself and your memories.

Feelings of guilt

A manipulator must be the king or queen of the victim. Instead of displaying direct aggressive behavior, they may choose to use passive aggression. An example of this might be something like, "It's okay to go out with your friends. I stay home alone and clean the house." This makes you feel bad, and they take on the role of the sensitive victim who has to do everything for you. Give up.

Ignore your problems

Rather than empathize with you and whatever issues you may be dealing with; a manipulator can use the time to talk about their issues. For example, suppose you complain about arguing with a family member. In that case, it could turn into a spiel about how at least you have one family to fight with or how their arguments with their relatives are much more common, for which you should be grateful.

Don't use their words.

Instead of talking to you about something that is bothering them, a manipulator may talk behind your back or use other passive-aggressive solutions. They may give you a silent treatment, pout or show procedures.

A definitive objective of influence is to persuade the objective to disguise the enticing contention and receive this new mentality, not do anything about it. When they are upset, they want to make sure everyone knows it. They can do something to show this to make people try to feel better. It can lead to a very exhausting and oppressive atmosphere to deal with, especially if it happens frequently.

Anger and aggression

Bullying is something many manipulative people rely on. This can be in the form of anger, hidden threats, or aggressive actions or language. This is all the truer when the manipulating party knows that the other does not like confrontation. Providing them with anxiety and discomfort will allow them to do whatever it takes to make the situation more comfortable, which usually means doing what they wanted in the first place.

Looking for trust

Handlers are often looking for insecure, sensitive, or trusting people. They know that these people are more vulnerable to manipulation and less likely to end it. By being kind and considerate, but gradually becoming more manipulative, they can begin to exploit the person, who is probably already attached to them and

handling techniques:

Lying: It is difficult to tell if someone is lying when they do, although the truth is often clarified later when it is too late. One way to minimize the chance of being lied to is to understand that some personality types (especially psychopaths) are adept at lying and cheating by doing so often and in subtle ways.

Lying by omission: This is a very subtle way to lie by hiding a significant part of the truth. This technique is also used in propaganda.

Denial: The manipulator refuses to admit that he has done something wrong.

Rationalization: An excuse from the manipulator for inappropriate behavior. Streamlining is closely related to spin.

Minimization - This is a type of denial combined with rationalization. The manipulator argues that his behavior is not as harmful or irresponsible as someone else suggested, for example, saying that a tease or insult was just a joke.

Selective inattention or selective attention: The manipulator refuses to pay attention to anything that might distract him from his schedule by saying things like "I don't want to hear it."

Distraction: manipulative who does not give a clear answer to a direct question, but rather distracts and redirects the conversation to another topic.

Evasion: Similar to distraction, but with vague and irrelevant answers, weasel words.

Hidden harassment: manipulative who puts the victim on the defensive through disguised threats (subtle, indirect or implicit).

Guilt - a special kind of intimidation tactic. A manipulator suggests to the conscious victim that they don't care enough, are too selfish, or have it easy. This generally makes the victim feel bad, leaving her in an insecure, fearful, and submissive position.

Insulting the victim: More than any other, this tactic is a powerful means of defending the victim while masking the handler's aggressive intentions.

Playing the part of a servant: Disguising a selfish agenda under the guise of service to a higher cause, such as saying that you are acting in a certain way out of "obedience" and "service" to God or some similar authority figure.

Temptation: The manipulator uses charm, praise, or open support from others to lower their defenses and show their trust and loyalty.

Projecting Guilt (Blaming Others) - The manipulator's scapegoat in ways that are often subtle and hard to discover.

Feigning Innocence: Manipulator attempts to imply that all the harm caused was unintentional or failed to do something he was accused of. The manipulator may appear shocked or outraged. This tactic causes the victim to question their judgment and possibly their own mental health.

Feign Confusion - The manipulator tries to play dumb by pretending that they don't know what you are talking about or are confused about a major issue reported to them.

Wielding Anger: The manipulator uses anger to swing with enough emotional intensity and anger to shock the victim and subdue them. The manipulator is not angry; he is just performing an act. He wants what he wants and gets "mad" when it is denied.

Manipulators exploit vulnerabilities.

Handlers exploit the following vulnerabilities (buttons) that can affect victims:

- addiction to gaining approval and acceptance from others

- Emetophobia (fear of negative emotions)

- lack of assertiveness and the ability to say no

- blurred sense of identity (with soft personal boundaries)

- low self-sufficiency

- external locus of control

naive: it is too difficult for the victim to accept the idea that some people are cunning, cunning, ruthless or "in denial" when they are victims

excessive anxiety: the victim is too willing to give the manipulator the benefit of the doubt and see their side of things where they blame the victim

Low self-esteem: The victim is self-doubtful, lacks self-confidence and assertiveness, and is likely to be overly defensive.

Over-intellectualization: the victim tries too hard to understand and believes that the manipulator has a legitimate and understandable reason to harm.

Emotional dependency: the victim has a submissive or dependent personality. The more emotional the victim, the more vulnerable they are to exploitation and manipulation.

Handlers generally take the time to identify their victim's characteristics and vulnerabilities.

- histrionic personality disorder

- passive-aggressive behavior

- type A angry personalities

- antisocial personality disorder

- addictive personalities.

Ways to deal with manipulation

Understand and be aware of what is happening around you. Please read the above material again and look for the things mentioned to know how to spot them next time. Be aware of how manipulation works and where it leads.

Listen to yourself and your feelings. When you doubt yourself or feel confused, keep that in mind and consider why you feel that way. Please pay attention to what the manipulative person does or says and how it affects you.

Pay more attention to actions than words. Please do not assume that when someone says something is the truth; otherwise, they will act accordingly. Instead, pay attention to what someone else is doing and base your feelings on that.

Understand that you are not a problem. If you realize that you are being manipulated, it is not your fault. Note that you did nothing wrong to cause it, and the other person has problems of their own. However, don't let this lead you to sympathy, but only to awareness.

Be assertive with yourself. Begin by choosing to stop responding to techniques as you did before. Say no if you want, talk if you want. Please understand that your answer is not your responsibility.

Think about the relationship with the other person. Maybe you want to talk to your friends about how you feel or want to confront the person. Consider all the options, and do what you want.

Regain your power by facing them. Only do this if you don't think you are in danger. But explaining how you feel and what bothers you is not a bad thing. Ask the other person to change their behavior. Don't let them continue with the same behavior. Get your strength back and do what you have to do.bv v

DARK NLP

What is Neurolinguistic Programming?

Neuro-linguistic programming, or NLP, offers practical ways to change the way you think you have studied, review past events, and focus on your lifestyle. Neuro-linguistic programming shows you how to take control of your mind and thus your existence. Unlike psychoanalysis, which makes the "why" a specialty, NLP is very sensitive and specialized in the "how."

Taking control of your mind: the principle behind NLP

NLP works from the beginning, now you have no control over your life, but you can most of the time deal with what is happening.

Your thoughts, feelings and emotions are not possible or that you have, regardless of the things you do. For example, their reasons can often be very complex in connection with comments or beliefs of your mother and father or teachers, or events that you have experienced.

NLP shows you how to manipulate those ideals and affection. Using visual thinking strategies, you can change how you think and experiment beyond events, fears, and even phobias.

The power of faith

What you agree with can be extremely powerful.

When you consider that you are sick and will die, you probably will: healers have used this approach for centuries.

Similarly, if you agree with what you had to do to improve, you often improve. This "placebo impact" has been well documented in clinical studies.

The bottom line is that if you think you can do something, you possibly can. But you can also go on a mission to prescribe ideals and exchange whether or not you can do something confident by asking yourself questions like:

How do I know that I can't try this?

Who told me that? Could they have been wrong?

Set goals

We are all familiar with goal setting standards, but NLP suggests some new and interesting ideas, specializing in pride, not dissatisfaction.

For example, it is good that your dreams are positive, knowledge of what you want to have, not what you would like to lose or not have now. It would be top-notch in case you also have an idea of what you want. For example, you don't have to buy your dream home. You have to live in it. It is much easier to be inspired by a goal that satisfies you.

The power of questions

Bandler shows that our mind actively seeks answers to questions.

So, if you ask yourself, "Why am I enjoying it so much?" Your thoughts will find many answers, and you will feel worse. With NLP, the secret is to ask the right questions, for example:

- Why do I want to change?

- What will the lifestyle be like after it changes?

- What do I have to do more / much less to change?

- Questions like these lead to a more beautiful view.

Moving pictures

Imagine a photo of someone who bothers you. Focus on how the photo looks in your mind.

Shrink the photo, put it in black and white, and imagine moving away from you. See how you experience this.

Imagine a picture of something that makes you feel amazing. Make it bigger and brighter and bring it closer to you. See how this makes you feel.

The concept behind this notion process is that it allows you to see how people or events affect you and recognize how you think about them.

By manipulating photos in this way, you teach your mind to exaggerate the right emotions and weaken the bad emotions.

Undermining the critical voice

Many of us will admit that we have a vital voice in our heads that pops up at inopportune times and says things like "You probably couldn't do this" or "That sounds too difficult for someone like you."

Notice how this changes the way you view the "know-how" of the voice. If the voice doesn't seem real, it's much less difficult to silence it.

Reverse the film

If you've had a horrible experience that you're going through to recover from, it can help take it backward.

Start with a factor in how long you realized the experience ended. Then consider the whole incident playing back in reverse until you go back to a time before it happened.

Do this several times until you understand how the "movie" plays backward.

Now make it small in your head, say enough to see a cell phone screen, and play it again.

Finally, consider another quit for pleasure, one that makes you smile. Notice how roughly the way you feel has changed.

This method's key is to show your brain a separate way to search for memory to change the way you feel about it.

"Brilliance squared."

Take an emotion that you would like to feel, such as self-confidence. Imagine a rectangle of color full of shadows that you associate with that emotion.

Imagine your state in the square, full of that emotion. Notice how you will stand, how your face will look, around you.

Enter the rectangular and take the mantle of the imaginary "you." Feel the sensation spreading through you. Repeat this several times until you can do it without problems.

Now imagine the colored square in front of you and go into it. See how it feels.

The "trick" here is that you have taught your mind to combine a photo with feeling. By calling the photo, you can now also evoke the feeling.

conclusion

NLP is a totally powerful method based on the power of your mind. Some may call it "thought suggestions," but by using those strategies and others developed through NLP practitioners, you can discover ways to take control of your mind and how it responds to the world.

You may not be in control of the world, but you can control how you react to it.

HOW TO USE REVERSE PSYCHOLOGY TO GET WHAT YOU WANT

You've probably done it countless times. And you may not even know you are doing it. "That" is reverse psychology. Reverse psychology is a simple concept. You want someone to do something, but you're pretty sure they won't, even if you ask nicely. So, you try to trick the person by asking or telling them to do the exact opposite of what you want them to do. For example, you are trying to get your husband to paint your bedroom without success. Then you say to him: "It doesn't matter, I'll do the bedroom, I'm a better painter anyway." Before you know it, he has a brush in hand.

Many people associate reverse psychology with children. For example, what parent has not told a teenager with purple hair that the color works for him, hoping that he will immediately dye it to his original color? But people of all ages are susceptible to its effects.

Reverse psychology often works because people need independence, says Dr. Jeanette Raymond, a licensed Los Angeles-based psychologist, therapist and relationship expert. "It is more powerful to think that you have done something of your own free will than because you have been forced, threatened, embarrassed or afraid of losing that relationship."

In the psychotherapeutic field, reverse psychology is more precisely known as a paradoxical intervention. (The term "reverse psychology" is a media invention, says Raymond.) In a paradoxical intervention, a therapist tells a client to display a behavior that the client is trying to resolve. So if a patient is trying to stop being a procrastinator, their counselor may tell them to spend an hour every day procrastinating. The idea is that this will help the client to focus on the behavior and its possible causes and will show that the behavior is voluntary and therefore, can be controlled.

The Best Ways to Use Reverse Psychology in Everyday Life

Kindly don't peruse this article as you are likely not shrewd enough to get it. Do you see what I did there? That was a basic case of an intricate marvel called invert brain research.

Invert brain science is an influence method

In general, people tend to do the opposite of what they are told. You are not the only one who broke your mother's rules as a child or climbed onto the construction site near your parent's house with the text 'STAY AWAY'.

However, it's not just about being told what to do. People also tend to find a more desirable option when discovering that it is no longer available or will not be available soon.

We want what we cannot have.

This is why playing hard to get works so well for dating.

Woman plays hard to get

For what reason accomplishes switch brain science work in so various situations?

Switch brain science works in regular day to day existence in various manners. Advisors use it with safe patients. Examiners use it to extricate admissions from lawbreakers. Guardians use it to cause their kids to keep the house rules. People use it to cause their accomplices to do anything they desire. Furthermore, sales reps utilize switch brain research to close arrangements quicker.

Invert brain science is a method for empowering a specific activity or communicating a specific conviction, which is something contrary to what you need.

It works for many people, especially those who like to be in control or are naturally resilient. There is a great deal of content out there on how reverse psychology is unethical and manipulative. But we will talk about ethics later.

In fact, with reverse psychology comes the appeal of authenticity. If someone feels they are not being told what to do, the interaction feels more fun and authentic.

Most people hate it being sold or being told to some line. This is why reverse psychology works. The reverse psychology technique is based on the predictable psychological phenomenon of reactance.

What is reactance, and why is reverse psychology based on it?

Reactance is a negative emotional response to being "sold" or persuaded that arises from people's natural resistance to being controlled or manipulated.

Reactance occurs in people who feel that agency is being taken away from them or that their options are limited.

For example, reactance can occur because an aggressive seller tries to get you to choose a particular stock. Reactivity can also occur when a particular rule or regulation is applied that restricts your freedom. Why do you think people like to break the rules so much?

When national parks have areas demarcated with a "Do Not Enter" sign, this only makes visitors want to enter the restricted area.

Depending on how someone has been raised, they will be naturally docile or resilient. You probably don't need to use reverse psychology for a very nice or accommodating person, as they will be more likely to agree to your requests or appreciate your suggestions.

Companies often use reverse psychology to sell their products. They make their products appear exclusive, limited edition, low in stock, or not currently available. This leads consumers to demand even more of the product.

Common examples of reverse psychology in everyday life

Imagine a mother trying to get her child to eat her broccoli. She can easily succeed by telling her child, "I would give you ice cream for dessert, but only after eating your broccoli. However, I don't think you can eat your broccoli. "

Suddenly, your son is on a mission to eat her broccoli because she was told she couldn't.

Imagine that you are a student trying to decide which courses to take. Any course that is already full and has a waiting list automatically looks more attractive. The psychology behind this coincides with the fear of missing out, popularly known as FOMO.

Speaking of college students, do you remember high school? Remember when your friends told you that you are probably too good to do something and made you want to do it?

Reverse psychology is also often used by personal trainers or sports coaches to encourage athletes to step up their game. Statements such as "You will have to train every day if you want to win this race and I don't think you have the self-discipline to do it," make the athlete want to train every day.

Similarly, when an athlete is told, "You are probably not going to win this race," he is even more motivated to secure victory.

Personal trainer motivating a client

The most common examples of reverse psychology in everyday life are examples of its use in dating and relationships. You've probably seen enough evidence that is playing hard to get works when you're dating. Remember, playing hard to get it is essentially reverse psychology.

Reverse Psychology in Dating and Relationships

We've all heard the story of the guy who proposed to his girlfriend because she suddenly seemed casual about whether to get engaged or not. We also heard the story of the girl who got her ex-boyfriend back by pretending she moved on and wasn't interested in reconnecting.

Annoying relationships never work out because most people don't like being told what to do.

Husband scolding his wife

The guy bullied by his girlfriend for not cheating is more likely than the guy who never hears a beep of concern about cheating on his girlfriend. I recently heard a story about a woman who got her boyfriend to stop cheating by proposing an open relationship where he could be with as many women as he wanted. Suddenly being with other women lost its appeal.

And what about the psychology behind being available when you're dating? Someone is too available in the early stages of a relationship is unattractive is the same reason you are not attracted to the product of a salesperson who seems desperate to make the sale.

People are more drawn to the things they have to work for, rather than the things they get easily or the things they are forced to do.

Giving your partner the silent treatment, turning your back, or playing hard to get it are also exampling of reverse psychology. If your partner maltreats you, this type of reverse psychology can motivate them to treat you better.

Famous examples of reverse psychology

In the classic 90s Disney movie Aladdin, Aladdin uses reverse psychology to trick the Ghost into helping him escape from the Cave of Wonders, without using any of his three wishes. He hints that the Ghost probably doesn't have the strength to pull them out of the cave. This, of course, causes the Ghost to prove Aladdin wrong. So, Aladdin gets what he wants: he gets Genie to help him escape the cage without using any of his wishes.

In another famous Disney movie, The Lion King, Scar tells Simba that only the bravest lions dare to visit the elephant graveyard. Scar knew that Simba's ego would motivate him to visit the cemetery.

Reverse Psychology in Advertising

Reverse psychology, pull marketing, or anti-marketing is becoming increasingly popular in the digital advertising space. Why? Because it works.

A few months ago, I saw an ad on Facebook saying goodbye to a city restaurant. He said the restaurant would close its doors at the end of the month and close.

Suddenly everyone wanted to make a reservation to eat at this restaurant. If it was a reverse psychology marketing tactic, it worked. It is suspicious that the doors of this restaurant are still open and have not closed.

I've seen billboard ads that say things like "Don't buy our product," and I have to admit they get my attention.

Commercial advertisement with reverse psychology messages

A famous advertisement for the outerwear brand Patagonia used reverse psychology and the caption "Don't buy this jacket." The ad encouraged online shoppers to buy only what they needed, keeping sustainability in mind. Ads like this made Patagonia look like an ethical and eco-friendly company that only made its products more attractive.

Ethical use of reverse psychology

If I told you that you probably can't do something to motivate yourself to prove me wrong, is it unethical? No. This type of reverse psychology is not unethical. Why? Because if someone is motivated to prove me wrong, they will perform better. They will also become better versions of themselves by invoking more drive and self-motivation.

Also, in sales, when you reinforce the prospect's autonomy by letting them know to make a choice, it is reverse ethical psychology. If you say something like "Whatever you decide, it's fine, it's your choice," they are more likely to want to work with you because you are not pushy.

Reverse psychology doesn't have to be used by everyone, as some people are naturally more complacent or agreeable.

In relationships, an example of ethical reverse psychology is telling your junk food junkie partner that you can eat as much junk food as you want. That's right; you don't care anymore if they ruin your health.

Saying this to someone who has resisted change when whining has not worked is an example of using reverse psychology for the greater good. This statement of yours will encourage introspection, where your partner will think about their bad eating habits and want to change.

"Positive manipulation" in therapy with resistant patients

A therapist who uses reverse psychology to help his patients change their unhealthy habits is another example of ethical practice.

A therapist might ethically use the reverse psychology method by telling someone who procrastinates too long to schedule time each week to procrastinate what they want.

Similarly, a patient with paralyzing anxiety and disturbing thoughts can be told to schedule 30 minutes from 8:00 p.m. at 8:30 p.m. every day to allow himself

/ herself to have those 30 minutes of anxious thoughts. What often happens is that the patient thinks of positive things during those 30 minutes.

Unethical use of reverse psychology

When reverse psychology works on you, and then you get upset that you've been misled, it can seem slimy or unethical.

This kind of trick is unethical and can give consumers a bad taste for the brand. What if you canceled very important dinner plans to finalize your online purchases because you thought this two-hour time limit was legitimate?

Another example of the unethical use of reverse psychology is when it comes to major threats. For example, you shouldn't threaten to break up with your partner to get him to do something you want.

Reverse psychology is ethical when it challenges people or companies to improve.

In many cases, reverse psychology is not only ethical, but it also leads to the positive transformation of a person.

If I were to use reverse psychology with you telling you that you probably can't do something, causing you to stop at nothing to prove me wrong, would you blame me for using reverse psychology on you? Would you think that I am manipulative? Probably not. The truth is, if what I said challenged you to get better and better, you will probably appreciate it. I would appreciate it if I was smart enough to use reverse psychology on you.

Are you motivated quickly? Or do you need reverse psychology to motivate you? If the latter sounds like you, then reverse psychology is a good thing.

The simple truth is that reverse psychology works for many of us, like it or not, and encourages us to do better. In other words, if we don't feel pressured by someone else, we decide to put pressure on ourselves.

Similarly, a company told it couldn't take it to the next level is suddenly motivated to increase brand awareness and become more known.

How to use reverse psychology

Reverse psychology refers to someone else doing or saying something by telling you the opposite of what you want. It can be very successful in advertising and can help deal with certain types of people. However, you must be very careful about how and when to use reverse psychology. It can be seen as a form of manipulation. With normal use, it can even damage relationships. Use reverse psychology only occasionally and in non-serious situations.

Change your mind with reverse psychology.

Start by presenting an option. Incorporate this option into the other person's brain. It can be something the person would normally resist, and they may tease it at first. However, it would help if you made sure that the person is aware of the available option.

Suppose you decide on a Friday night between two parties. Your boyfriend is a movie buff, and his group of friends is having a movie night. You are more of a board game, and another group of friends has a game night.

Notify your friend of the option you want. Say something like, "Did you hear Madison and Emily do board game night? Pretty boring, if you ask me."

Also, use non-verbal cues. For example, you can play a version of a board game on your phone in front of the person. You could invite Madison and Emily over for coffee with the other person at the party, reminding them how nice they are.

Use subtle shapes to make the option attractive. Find ways to make the option desirable. Leave subtle suggestions that can create a sense of desire in the other person.

In the example above, you can casually mention the board games played during the event. You can also play cards with your friends a few days before the event so that your friend can see how much fun games can be.

It can also make friends appear more attractive. Bring back some great memories you had with Madison and Emily. Talk about their good qualities. For example, say something like, "Madison always has the best selection of wines in her house."

Discourage or dispute the option you want. Once the person becomes addicted, you will want to argue a bit. This will give you the extra boost you need to get the person to do what you want. They are already somewhat tempted by the option. If you decline that option at this point, a naturally resistant person will likely push you further.

Going back to the previous example, wait until Friday night arrives. Say something like, "Well, we can go to Madison and Emily, or that movie night. What do you think? I think Madison and Emily might be a little boring."

At this point, your friend can push to go to Madison and Emily. However, if they are still ambivalent, try to be more open. Say something like, "We can always go with Madison and Emily at another time."

Push the person to make a decision. To close the negotiation process, you can now pressure the person to make a decision. The idea here is to make the person believe that they are making their own decision. Politely ask them what they want to do and wait for a response. Hopefully, the person will choose the option they competed for.

In the example above, say something like, "Then we can go to Madison and Emily's, or the movies. What do you think? It's your decision."

Making your friend believe that it is his decision will make him think that he is claiming his autonomy. You already made Madison and Emily's party look seductive. She has also expressed some resistance to it, which a naturally opposite person can resist. Hopefully, your friend will pick Madison and Emily's event.

Find situations in which reverse psychology is effective.

Find out which personality types respond best to reverse psychology. Not everyone responds well to reverse psychology. People who tend to be more compliant are better able to respond to direct requests. If you know someone who is naturally resistant, reverse psychology can work well for this person.

Think about the interactions you have had with the person. Do they float along with things, or do they will, in general, stand up to? On the off chance that you know somebody who is a freer mastermind and likes to oppose business as usual, this individual might be more inclined to invert brain science than somebody who is commonly affable.

Tip: You ought to likewise remember this on the off chance that you intend to utilize invert brain research in kids. If you have a youngster who will, in general, be obstinate, they are significantly more prone to react to turn around brain research than to a pleasant kid.

Focus on a light utilization of opposite brain science, particularly with youngsters. Switch brain research ought to be carefree and even fun. This is particularly evident when the method is utilized in extremely little youngsters. Attempt to utilize it as a way to make somebody imagine that they are outfoxing you.

Suppose you are trying to get your child to make the bed on time. You can ask her to wait to make her bed until she finishes brushing her teeth and explain that she is young and needs a lot of help. You may enter the room and find that she have already started the process alone because she want to demonstrate her autonomy.

Try using reverse psychology on an adult in the same way. Make the person think they are asserting their autonomy in the situation. Perhaps you choose between two films: a foreign film with subtitles versus a light-hearted comedy. You want to see the foreign movie, so you might say something like, "I'm not sure I have the subtitles' attention span." Your friend may be pushing for the foreign movie right now because he wants to demonstrate his superior attention span.

Think about what the other person wants. Before using reverse psychology, think about what the other person is likely to want in a situation. In some cases, a more complicated version of reverse psychology may be required. If someone wants to do something that outweighs their need to resist, classic reverse psychology can backfire. For example, your friend wants to go to a concert in a bad part of town. You may think this is a poorly conceived notion; however, utilizing basic opposite brain research can be ineffectual. If your state to your companion, "You're correct. You need to go. You just live once!" your companion may concur, as he truly needs to watch the show.

Don't abuse reverse psychology. Reverse psychology can work very well in certain situations. However, keep in mind that it is a subtle form of manipulation. In general, using reverse psychology can be incredibly damaging to relationships.

Minor situations like this can lead to overtime, which can lead to resentment in a relationship. For example, your partner may get tired of not getting his way and start to get mad at you.

Note: Use reverse psychology in low-risk situations. For example, you can use this tactic when you and your partner decide which movie to watch. However, please don't use it every time you watch a movie, as you will occasionally need to let your partner choose their recreational activities.

Stay calm when using reverse psychology. Reverse psychology can be frustrating, especially when used with children. Stubborn kids, and people in general, can take a while to get into their thinking. You want to stay calm and stay calm.

If your child is having an emotional outburst while using reverse psychology, stay calm. Let the child continue. With tolerance, your youngster should quiet down and act.

Try not to utilize turn around brain research in difficult circumstances. There are certain circumstances in which turn around brain research will probably reverse discharge, and the outcomes can be desperate. You ought to consistently cease utilizing reverse brain science when somebody's wellbeing and prosperity are in question.

Assume your companion has a constant dread of specialists. They have a dubious mole developing on their correct shoulder and are hesitant to get it looked at.

Don't say, "You're right. Don't go to the doctor." Your friend's fear of doctors can far outweigh his need to resist, and you can reinforce dangerous behavior.

In these cases, try to go against yourself, rather than the choice that is before you. Going back to the previous model, you can say something to your companion, similar to "I can't cause you to do anything you would prefer not to do. I'm almost certain some portion of the town is hazardous; however, no one but you can choose what to do." The best for you."

You urge your companion to think for himself here. If your companion is normally safe, you can surrender to their recommendation instead of having an independent mind. Your companion may choose not to go to the show.

Consider your ultimate objective. Ensure you remember your ultimate objective. Help yourself routinely to remember what you need the individual to do. Now and then, things can get troublesome on the off chance that you utilize invert brain research. It's easy to lose sight of your wishes in an argument. Try to stay the course and remember the desired result.

Avoid misuse of reverse psychology.

HOW TO OVERCOME MANIPULATION

Reasons We Allow Ourselves to Be Manipulated

The only time when manipulation is considered auspicious is when you allow it to control your emotions and thoughts. Thus, you must start to distinguish what is going on in you that will enable you to be easily manipulated by other people.

The three most basic reasons we let ourselves to be manipulated are as follows:

Fear

This emotion comes in numerous structures. We, as human beings, tend to fear to lose a relationship; we may fear other people; we dread to make somebody discontent with our actions. We additionally dread the dangers and outcomes of the manipulator's activities. Imagine a scenario in which they prevail at doing what they threaten.

Guilt

Today, we are clouded by the idea and responsibility that we should dependably prioritize the needs and wants of other people rather than our own. At times when people would talk about the right to fulfill their individual needs and wants, manipulators frequently abuse and endeavor to make us feel like we are accomplishing something immoral if we do not generally put their needs and wants in front of our own. Those individuals who are skilled at these manipulative tactics would tend to define love as fulfilling their needs and wants as part of your obligation. Hence, if we have an opinion that goes against their beliefs, we are manipulated into thinking that we are heartless; at this point, they would make us feel very regretful of our existence and would use guilt to manipulate us.

Being too nice

We appreciate being a provider, fulfilling individuals, and dealing with the needs of other people. We discover fulfillment. Moreover, our confidence would regularly originate from doing what we can for other people. In any case, at times when there is a lack of an unmistakable feeling of these and fair limitations, skilled manipulators can detect this in people who are easy targets of this phenomenon and will use specific tactics to further their selfish gains.

What You Need to Do to Overcome Manipulation

We have come to a point where we are here to talk about the necessary skills to overcome manipulation. Moreover, manipulation would only work if you allow them to control you. We will discuss some of the essential techniques to overcome manipulation, which is as follows:

Establish a clear sense of self

There is a need to know your identity, your needs, and wants your emotions and what you are fond of and not fond of. You must learn to accept these and not become apologetic, as these are the things that make you. At times, we dread that in the event of speaking up, we are viewed by others as egotistical and called out for being selfish. Nevertheless, knowing your identity or what you need in life is not an act of selfishness. Self-centeredness is demanding that you always get what you want or that other has always put your needs and wants first. Similarly, when another person calls you out for not following their orders or fulfilling their needs and wants, they are selfish, not you.

Say "no" despite the other person's disapproval

The ability to say "no" despite somebody's objection is a solid demonstration. Individuals who can do this are present in reality. Because in fact, there is no way that we can accommodate all of their needs and wants. When this happens, they will become baffled, even disappointed. However, keep in mind that what they are feeling is part of human nature. Most of these individuals would then forgive and forget. Sound individuals realize that getting what you want all the time is impossible, even when the desires are genuine. In any case, when we cannot endure another person's mistake or objection, it ends up hard, stating "no." It winds up more diligently for us to declare it or have limits. Manipulators exploit this shortcoming and use dissatisfaction and objection in extraordinary structures to get us to do what they need.

Tolerate the other person's negative affect

We can demonstrate compassion for people's pity, hurt, or even annoyance when accommodating without needing to back down and reverse our decision. Keep in mind, a stable relationship is described by common minding, shared genuineness, and shared regard. If you are involved with somebody who uses manipulation and unhealthy control consistently, begin to see little propensities that may not be clear to you at first. As you are more grounded, you are better ready to endure how the other individual's negative impact on you is only bringing you down. Thus, this turns into a positive development that liberates you from their manipulative grasps. It will engender a complexity of sorts with the people in your life. The manipulator may start to withdraw and consider your time, emotions, wants, and needs, or proceed onward to someone else who is an easy target of manipulation practices.

Basic Tricks Used By Manipulators

As soon as you have realized how knowledge of certain truths about yourself can enlighten you to notice manipulative tactics by other people, you will start to divulge from what you are to what a manipulator can do. With that in mind, if you wish to overcome manipulation, you need to be wary of the primary tactics used by manipulators. Once you have a firm grasp as to what you want and what you do not wish to, you can go head-to-head with a manipulator and even counter some of their most-used techniques. Nevertheless, always keep in mind that as soon as you realize that you are being manipulated, the manipulator loses. It is merely a matter of whether you wish to turn the tables and become the manipulator yourself.

Accusing your rival of what he is blaming you for

It is often referred to as the act of pointing to another person's wrongdoing. When enduring an onslaught and experiencing difficulty regarding safeguarding themselves, manipulators tend to reverse the situation. They blame their rival for committing the exact things that they are being blamed for. "You state that I don't love you! I think it is you who does not cherish me!"

Appealing to power

Numerous individuals are in wonderment of those in power or authority, or those who have status. What's more intriguing is that there are various images to which individuals experience extraordinary dedication. Remember, those who are easily manipulated admire those who are in power. Moreover, those in power are aware of their ability to control others by never criticizing them. Instead, they use sophisticated misleading tactics to maneuver their thoughts and alter their decision-making process.

Appealing to encounter

Gifted manipulators and con artists, as well as politicians, would often state that they already have experienced or encountered certain situations in their life, which makes them someone who is in power, which can be associated with the point. Nevertheless, this appeal to experience provides them with an image of someone capable; this may be used to attack their opponent's lack of knowledge, even though they have limited expertise. You can quickly identify this manipulation tactic at times when someone is trying to distort their capabilities about a particular subject.

Appealing to fear

People have fears. The unscrupulous manipulators realize a reality that individuals will, in general, respond crudely when any of these feelings of dread are enacted. Subsequently, they speak to themselves as being able to ensure individuals against these dangers, even when they are not capable of doing so. It is the same for when we talked about giving the target a glimpse of how their most desired outcome is achievable, without providing it to them. Nonetheless, politicians and legislators frequently utilize this methodology to ensure that individuals line up behind administrative experts and do what the legislature – that is, the thing that the government officials need.

Appealing to sympathy

Manipulators can depict themselves and their circumstances to the public in a means to make them feel frustrated about their current situation.

Utilization of this ploy empowers the manipulator to occupy consideration from those individuals who may be going through the same thing. Nevertheless, appealing to sympathy is a tactic that most politicians would use to redirect the public's attention to matters that do not affect their demise.

Appealing to well-known interests

Manipulators and tricksters are always mindful as to how they introduce themselves as persons who possess the right qualities and perspectives among the group of spectators, particularly the sacred beliefs of the crowd. Everybody has a few partialities, and a great many people feel contempt toward a person or thing.

Appealing to confidence

This technique is firmly identified with past points. Yet, it stresses what appears to have breezed through the trial of time. Individuals are regularly oppressed by the social traditions and standards of their way of life, just as social conventions. What is conventional to most tend to appear as if it is the correct decision? You must note that manipulators infer how they regard sacred the ideologies and beliefs that the group of spectators is familiar with. These individuals suggest that their enemy aims to obliterate the customs, as well as social conventions.

Moreover, they do not stress over whether or not these conventions hurt guiltless individuals. They make the presence of being autonomous from the crowd's perspectives; yet, but it would typically be the exact opposite. There is a realization that individuals are generally suspicious of the individuals who conflict with existing social standards and built up conventions. They realize enough to stay away from these. As a result, there is a kind of restriction on how social traditions are unwittingly and carelessly bound.

Creating a false dilemma

A genuine problem happens when we are compelled to pick between two similarly unsuitable choices. A false dilemma occurs when we are convinced that we have just two, equally inadmissible decisions when we genuinely have multiple potential outcomes accessible to us. Think about the accompanying case: "Either we will lose the war on terrorism, or we should surrender a portion of our traditional freedoms and rights."

Individuals are frequently prepared to acknowledge a false dilemma since few are agreeable with the complex qualifications. Clearing absolutes is a part of their manipulative tactics. There is a need to have clear and essential decisions.

Hedging what you state

Manipulators frequently hole up behind words, declining to submit themselves or give straightforward replies or answers. It enables them to withdraw at times of need. They would think of another reason for not being able to come up with said information whenever they found forgetting data significant to the current situation. At the end of the day, when forced, they may be able to give in; however, to be an excellent manipulator, you should renege on your missteps, conceal your mistakes, and gatekeeper what you state at whatever point conceivable.

Oversimplifying the issue

Since most people are uncomfortable at comprehending profound or unobtrusive contentions, they are fond of oversimplifying the issue to further their potential benefit. "I couldn't care less what the measurements inform us concerning the purported abuse of detainees; the main problem is whether we will be tough on crime. Spare your compassion toward the criminals' victims, not for the actual criminals." The reality being overlooked is that the maltreatment of criminals is a crime in itself. Tragically, individuals with an over-simple mindset could not care less about criminal conduct that victimizes criminals.

BEHAVORAL TRAITS OF FAVORITE VICTIMS OF MANIPULATOR

Specific characteristics and behavioral traits make people more vulnerable to manipulation, and people with dark psychology traits know this full well. They tend to seek out victims who have those specific behavioral traits because they are necessarily easy targets. Let's discuss 6 of the characteristics of the favorite victims of manipulators.

Emotional Insecurity and Fragility

Manipulators like to target victims who are emotionally insecure or emotionally fragile. Unfortunately for these victims, such traits are easy to identify even in total strangers, so it's easy for experienced manipulators to find them.

Emotionally insecure people tend to be defensive when they are attacked or under pressure, which makes them easy to spot in social situations. Even after a few interactions, a manipulator can gauge a certain degree of accuracy and how insecure a person is. They'll try to provoke their potential targets subtly, and then wait to see how they react. If they are overly defensive, manipulators will take it as a sign of insecurity, and they will intensify their manipulative attacks.

Manipulators can also tell if a target is emotionally insecure if he/she redirects accusations or negative comments. They will find a way to put you on the spot, and if you try to throw it back at them, or to make excuses instead of confronting the situation head-on, the manipulator could conclude that you are insecure and therefore an easy target.

People who have social anxiety also tend to have emotional insecurity, and manipulators are aware of this. In social gatherings, they can easily spot individuals who have social anxiety, then target them for manipulation. "Pickup artists" can identify the girls who seem uneasy in social situations by the way they conduct themselves.

Emotional fragility is different from emotional insecurity. Emotionally insecure people tend to show it all the time, while emotionally fragile people appear to be healthy, but they break down emotionally at the slightest provocation. Manipulators like targeting emotionally sensitive people because it's straightforward to elicit a reaction from them. Once a manipulator finds out that you are emotionally vulnerable, he will jump at the change to manipulate you because he knows it would be reasonably accessible.

Emotional fragility can be temporary, so people with these traits are often targeted by opportunistic manipulators. People may be emotionally stable most of the time. Still, he/she may experience emotional fragility when they are going through a breakup, when they are grieving, or when they are dealing with a situation that is emotionally draining. The more diabolical manipulators can earn your trust, bid their time, and wait for you to be emotionally fragile.

Sensitive People

Highly sensitive people are those individuals who process information at a deeper level and are more aware of the subtleties in social dynamics. They have lots of positive attributes because they tend to be very considerate of others, and they watch their step to avoid causing people any harm, whether directly or indirectly. Such people tend to dislike any form of violence or cruelty, and they are easily upset by news reports about disastrous occurrences, or even depictions of gory scenes in movies.

Sensitive people also tend to get emotionally exhausted from taking in other people's feelings. When they walk into a room, they have the immediate ability to detect other people's moods, because they are naturally skilled at identifying and interpreting other people's body language cues, facial expressions, and tonal variations.

Manipulators like to target sensitive people because they are easy to manipulate. If you are sensitive to certain things, manipulators can use them against you. They will feign certain emotions to draw vulnerable people so that they can exploit them.

Sensitive people also tend to scare easily. They have a heightened "startle reflex," which means that they are more likely to show clear signs of fear or nervousness in potentially threatening situations. For example, sensitive people are more likely to jump up when someone sneaks up on them, even before they determine whether they are in any real danger. This trait can be complicated to hide if you are a sensitive person, and malicious people will be able to see it from a mile away.

Sensitive people also tend to be withdrawn. They are mostly introverts, and they like to keep to themselves because social stimulation can be emotionally draining for them. Manipulators who are looking to control others are more likely to target people who are introverted because that trait makes it easy to isolate potential victims.

Manipulators can also identify sensitive people by listening to how they talk. Vulnerable people tend to be very proper; they never use vulgar language, and they tend to be very politically correct because they are trying to avoid offending anyone. They also tend to be polite, and they say "please" and "thank you" more often than others. Manipulators go after such people because they know that they are too polite to dismiss them right away; sensitive people will indulge anyone because they don't want to be rude, and that gives people maliciously away in.

Emphatic People

Emphatic people are generally similar to highly sensitive people, except that they are more attuned to the feelings of others and the energy of the world around them. They tend to internalize other people's suffering to the point that it becomes their own. In fact, for some of them, it can be difficult to distinguish someone's discomfort from their own. Emphatic people make the best partners because they feel everything you feel. However, this makes them particularly easy to manipulate, which is why malicious people like to target them.

Malicious people can feign certain emotions, and convey those emotions to emphatic people, who will feel them as though they were real. That opens them up for exploitation. Emphatic people are the favorite targets of psychopathic conmen because they feel so deeply for others. A conman can make up stories about financial difficulties and swindle lots of money from emphatic people.

The problem with being emphatic is that because you have such strong emotions, you easily dismiss your doubts about people because you would much instead offer help to someone who turns out to be a lair than deny support to someone who turns out to be telling the truth.

Emphatic people have a big-hearts, and they tend to be extremely generous, often to their detriment. They are highly charitable, and they feel guilty when others around them suffer, even if it's not their fault and can't do anything about it. Malicious people have an effortless time taking such people on guilt trips. They are the kind of people who would willingly fork over their life savings to help their friends get out of debt, even if it means they would be ruined financially.

Malicious people like to get into relationships with emphatic people because they are easy to take advantage of. Emphatic people try to avoid getting into intimate relationships in the first place because they know that it's easy for them to get engulfed in such links and lose their identities.

Fear of Loneliness

Many people are afraid of being alone, but this fear is heightened in a small percentage of the population. This kind of concern can be genuinely paralyzing for those who experience it, and it can open them up to exploitation by malicious people. Many people stay in dysfunctional relationships because they are afraid they will never find someone else to love them if they break up with an abusive partner. Manipulators can identify this fear in a victim, and they'll often do everything they can to fuel it further to make sure that the person is crippled by it. People who are afraid of being alone can tolerate or even rationalize any kind of abuse.

The fear of being alone can be easy to spot in a potential victim. People with this kind of anxiety tend to exude some level of desperation at the beginning of relationships, and they can sometimes come across as clingy. While ordinary people may think of being clingy as a red flag, manipulative people will see it as an opportunity to exploit somebody. If you are attached to them, they'll use manipulative techniques to make you even more dependent on them.

The fear of being alone is, for the most part, a social construct, and it disproportionately affects women more than men. For generations, our society has taught women that their goal in life is to get married and have children. Even the more progressive women who reject this social construct are still plagued by social pressures to adhere to those old standards.

People with abandonment issues stemming from childhood tend to experience the fear of loneliness to a higher degree. Some may not necessarily fear loneliness in general, but they are afraid of being separated from the essential people in their lives. For example, many people end up staying in abusive or dysfunctional relationships because they are so scared of being separated from their children.

Fear of Disappointing Others

We all feel a certain sense of obligation towards the people in our lives, but some are terrified of disappointing others. This kind of fear is similar to the fear of embarrassment or rejection. It means that the person puts a lot of stock into how others perceive him or her. The fear of disappointing others can occur naturally, and it can be useful in some situations; parents who are afraid of disappointing their families will work harder to provide for them, and children who are fearful of disappointing their parents will study harder at school. In this case, the fear is constructive. However, it becomes unhealthy when directed at the wrong people, or when it forces you to compromise your comfort and happiness.

When manipulators find out that you fear disappointing others, they'll try to put you in a position where you feel like you owe them something. They'll do individual favors for you, and then they'll manipulate you into believing that you have a sense of obligation towards them. They will then guilt you into complying with any request whenever they want something from you.

Personality Dependent Disorders and Emotional Dependency

Dependent personality disorder refers to a disease characterized by an excessive and even pervasive need to be taken care of. This need often leads the person to be submissive towards the people in their lives and to be clingy and afraid of separation. People with this disorder act in ways that are meant to elicit caregiving. They tend to practice what's called "learned helplessness."

This is where they act out of a conviction that they are unable to do certain things for themselves and need others' help.

Such people have a hard time making decisions, even when dealing with simple things like picking out which clothes to wear. They need constant reassurance and advice, and they let others take the lead in their own lives. These are the kinds of people who either move back into their parents' homes as adults or treat their spouses and partners as though they are their parents.

Manipulators like to target people with dependent personality disorders because they are straightforward to control and dominate. These people willingly cede control over their lives to others, so when manipulators come knocking, they don't face much resistance. Manipulators start by giving them a false sense of security, but once they have won their trust, they switch gears and start imposing their will on them.

Emotional dependency is similar to dependent personality disorder, but it doesn't rise to clinical significance. It stems from having low self-esteem, and it's often a result of childhood abandonment issues. They tend to be very agreeable because they want to please the people in their lives. Such people are easy to manipulate, and malicious people can easily dominate them.

CONCLUSION

Today, the opportunity has come to deduce from these observations that social principles, laws, and morals are actually 'commonplaces' for humans and that society consistently drives herd behavior on them, depending on the historical, of the desperate. Frankly, this persistence mentality is our standard, and society strives to control the wild mammoth in every person. Since its inception, it has been following the laws, rules and customs of the ruling assembly; when in doubt, the rich dominate our governing bodies and institutions.

That is the explanation we must do to ensure that people recognize that society is not offering them a sensible deal. What would be a smart thought for them in a time of hostile condition where their benefit depends on their school, their family, or their wealth? Psychology itself must come out of the warehouse and see that common human behavior must contradict fixed social rules and demands. Frankly, people are furious with society, but being weak against those who control institutions and morals, they feel powerless to hope to live among the sheep.

Is it surprising that a disconnected individual chooses to change society or their condition to live an increasingly free and controlled life over a ruthless society? As we've seen, does that eventually fall apart and present itself as the new rich and fantastic restorative force? In the main notable century, we have seen China evolve from a shopping-oriented area to a military framework controlled by the rich and dazzled, to a communist vision in the 1950s, when Marxism would choose a lonely life for all. In conclusion, as a corporate visionary communist state, China is subject to the choice of a social occasion that describes the life of an exposed people who have sincerely struggled to oversee the rulers as much as the emperor of recent years. - nothing has changed the wealthy and influential. Later there will be another uprising in China.

At the moment, it seems in all likelihood strange, despite unrest in various parts of China caused by minorities being forced to follow the central law. Not all domains can see them disappear! So how will psychology approach this issue of human behavior as a fundamental part of continuity, to be specific in the sense that people are often horrible, strict, and beat up others more powerless than themselves? Psychiatry in clinical psychiatric centers is commonly regarded as a technique of social control. If you don't agree with society and its standards, you should be crazy.

At this point, we must participate and have control over everyone's safety and preferred position. Psychology, for its part, has all the hallmarks to release part of the mental wealth: we help people who are out of tune with society to discover their place and discover behaviors that they consider normal at this time. Where will people who oppose the community in which they live and need a different lifestyle to react without being disturbed by wonder and the possibility of continuing the presence they choose for themselves? Or again, we believe that movies will become a reality, a disaster that all humans imagine, and appearances like a dog are called persistence, the true social standard!